WEREWOLVES
and
SHAPESHIFTERS

Darren Zenko

GHOST HOUSE

Ghost House Books

The Publisher: Ghost House Books
Distributed by Lone Pine Publishing

10145 – 81 Avenue	1808 – B Street NW, Suite 140
Edmonton, AB T6E 1W9	Auburn, WA 98001
Canada	USA

Website: http://www.ghostbooks.net

National Library of Canada Cataloguing in Publication

Zenko, Darren, 1974–
  Werewolves and shapeshifters / Darren Zenko.

  ISBN 1-894877-53-5

  1. Werewolves.   2. Metamorphosis—Folklore.   I. Title.
GR830.W4Z45 2004   398.24'54   C2004-901648-2

Editorial Director: Nancy Foulds
Project Editor: Chris Wangler
Illustrations, Cover: Aaron Norell
Production Manager: Gene Longson
Book Design, Layout & Production: Chia-Jung Chang
Cover Design: Gerry Dotto

The stories, folklore and legends in this book are based on the author's research. They are meant to entertain, and neither the publisher nor the authors claim these stories represent fact.

We acknowledge the financial support of the Government of Canada through the Book Publishing Industry Development Program (BPIDP) for our publishing activities.

PC: 5

For Shannon

Contents

Acknowledgments 5

Introduction 6

The Curse of Lycaon 12

The Wolf-Man 25

A Fox in the Cathouse 66

The Wendigo 97

Two Barrels of Silver 105

The Boto 142

The Beast of le Gévaudan 175

Acknowledgments

Thanks go first of all to everyone at Lone Pine who made this book possible—Chris "the Wrangler" Wangler, Nancy Foulds, Shane Kennedy, Chia-Jung Chang and Gerry Dotto. Here's to your patience. Thanks also to Aaron Norell, whose illustrations for this volume quite frankly rock.

Personal thanks go out to everybody who put up with me during this book's long and painful birth—my wonderful parents, Shannon O'Toole, Fish Griwkowsky, Dwayne Martineau, Stephen Notley...I could do this all day; you know who you are. Jon Pelster, Jody Cloutier, Paul Coutts and lycanthropological consultant Rod MacKinnon—thanks for the loan of some invaluable books. Speaking of which, I'd also like to compliment Jamie Hall, whose fine volume *Half Human, Half Animal* provided much folkloric background to the telling of the story of the Boto. For that matter, I must thank all the writers, folklorists and storytellers—professional or amateur—who keep these stories alive around the world.

Finally, thanks to all the waitresses and bartenders.

Introduction

"Werewolfery is of itself a vast subject, and when we quite legitimately extend our pervestigation to shape-shifting and animal metamorphosis in general the field is immense."
　　—Montague Summers, *The Werewolf,* 1933

"No matter how appealing, do not let strange creatures into your house! We all know strange creatures are on the increase. Many of them do seem furry and adorable. But beware! We know not from whence they came!"
　　—Alex Cox, *Repo Man*

We all know what a werewolf is, right? A guy who, when the full moon is up, turns into a man-wolf thing with a wolf's head and lower legs, hairy body, huge arms with nasty claws and teeth that'd make Little Red Riding Hood drop her basket and run. He prowls the moonlit night in his bloodlust, searching for human prey, and only silver bullets can kill him. He probably caught the curse through being bitten or scratched by another werewolf, and he can pass it on to others in the same way. Sound familiar?

That's the popular, modern "Hollywood" idea of the werewolf, anyway, but it's just one small part of the body of Western werewolf folklore. And Western werewolf folklore is just the tail-tip of the enormous worldwide folklore involving people who transform into wolves.

And all that global werewolf mythology is, in turn, but one element of the vast tradition of shapeshifting lore human cultures have created over the millennia.

Shapeshifter mythology is truly universal and unspeakably ancient. The oldest known work of human art, an ivory carving recently discovered in a cave near Blaubeuren in southwestern Germany, depicts a man in the process of transforming into a lion. This little carving, about the width of a fingernail, dates to 33,000 years ago, a time when early modern humans shared the earth with the rugged Neanderthals.

Not only are stories of human-animal transformation (and vice-versa, by the way) universal in the human experience, they are also ever-present in human space. No culture, anywhere on the planet, is lacking in tales of this sort. The Natives of North America are steeped in stories of legendary trickster figures—Old Man, Coyote, Whisaketchak and countless others—who constantly change their shape to teach (and learn) lessons and play tricks. In South America, there are were-dolphins and cat-people, while the cold lands of Scandinavia still ring with stories of the *berserkers,* crazed Norse warriors who charged into battle inflamed with the power of the bear or wolf skins they wore. Europe has thousands of variations on the werewolf legend, as well as those vampires that transform themselves into beasts, bats or vermin. In Africa, there are lion-men and were-hyenas who hold the secrets of blacksmithing. In ancient, magical India, treasures and sacred places are guarded by the serpent-people called Naga, and the demonic Rakshasa change their shape to torment mankind. Were-tigers lurk in Southeast Asia, while shapeshifting fox spirits tempt, test and torment the Japanese.

Just in case anybody is of the impression that these legends are somehow reserved for quaint tribal cultures, ancient histories, amusing fairy stories or dusty collections of interesting but unliving folklore, I must point out that the world's major religions are not exempt from the universality of the shapeshifter myth. Even that great source and center of Western spirituality, the Bible, has its fair share of transformation stories. Everyone knows, for example, the story of how Lot's wife was turned into a pillar of salt for looking back on the destruction of Sodom—though conversions into mineral form are a bit outside the scope of this book—but how many people remember how God humbled the proud Nebuchadnezzar, King of Babylon, by turning him for seven years into a sort of ox-man? It occurs in the fourth chapter of the Book of Daniel (in the King James version):

> 30 The king spake, and said, Is not this great Babylon, that I have built for the house of the kingdom by the might of my power, and for the honor of my majesty?

> 31 While the word was in the king's mouth, there fell a voice from heaven, saying, O king Nebuchadnezzar, to thee it is spoken; The kingdom is departed from thee.

> 32 And they shall drive thee from men, and thy dwelling shall be with the beasts of the field: they

shall make thee to eat grass as oxen, and seven times shall pass over thee, until thou know that the most High ruleth in the kingdom of men, and giveth it to whomsoever he will.

33 The same hour was the thing fulfilled upon Nebuchadnezzar: and he was driven from men, and did eat grass as oxen, and his body was wet with the dew of heaven, till his hairs were grown like eagles' feathers, and his nails like birds' claws.

As diverse and widespread as these stories may be, there are still unifying themes that extend across all cultures, and across all species of animals. For instance, there is the "retribution" angle, in which the curse of transformation is visited upon some human (or, again, some animal) by a god or other supernatural power as punishment for some terrible sin, or even some—to us—minor indiscretion. The ancient story of Lycaon, which I've included in this book, is one such story. The reverse example is also true, of course: often, a person who has been sinned against will, in legend, assume an animal or half-animal shape in order to become an instrument of punishment. The Blackfoot story of "The Wolf-Man," which I have also included here, follows this common pattern.

Some stories, from cultures separated by half a planet and thousands of years, hold so closely to a common pattern that it's almost scary. Consider the "sea-wife" legend, the most famous Western European version of which can be found in stories of the seal-women known as Selkies in the Orkney and Shetland Islands, and by dozens of other names throughout Europe. In these stories, the Selkie, in assuming human form to bask on the beach, sheds her magical sealskin. The precious skin is found by a fisherman, and he uses it to extort her into a marriage, which seldom ends happily. Some details may change, the species may change—in Japan, it is likely to be a fox-maiden; the Inuit tell stories of an unhappy goose woman—and even the genders may be reversed, but the plot, the rhythm, the nature of the magic stays the same, and has stayed the same since prehistoric times.

To call these deep currents of the human spirit "prehistoric" is, again, not to call them dead. Ancient, yes, but never dead. Consider the huge amount of recent popular interest in those most subtle of beast-people, the vampires, as shown by the success of TV shows such as *Buffy the Vampire Slayer* and movies such as *Blade*—or, more close to the traditional image of animal transformation, the growing resurgence of interest in werewolves in movies such as the inventive (and fittingly subversive) *Ginger Snaps* series. Consider, also, that every day of the week, all around the world, tens of thousands of people are acting out their primeval transformation fantasies in role-playing games like White Wolf Studios' *Werewolf: Apocalypse.* Say what you like, but if that's not a living folklore, what is?

This book was never intended to be an encyclopedia—there are already a huge number of excellent books of that type, and to add to the work of those folklorists is beyond my ability. Instead, my goal is to present a sampling of werewolf and shapeshifter legends from around the world in the form they were meant to appear in—as stories. These retellings are all fictional—or, I might say, all legendary—but they are based on extensive research into the folklore involved. Given the sheer variety of sources, I've taken a few different approaches.

Most of these stories—"The Wolf-Man," "A Fox in the Cathouse," "The Curse of Lycaon" and "The Wendigo"— take their storylines straight from legend, but have been recast into modern prose short stories. Two are original narratives meant to illustrate the folklore that inspired them: "The Boto" reveals the strange mythology of the Amazon were-dolphin through the eyes of a modern American woman, and "Two Barrels of Silver" is meant to put the "Western" back into Western werewolf lore. And one, "The Beast of le Gévaudan," is meant, through fact and fiction, to tell an important—and well-documented—French werewolf story in a form more accurate, detailed and entertaining than is usually found in English-language sources.

Above all, though, my goal has been to entertain. I can't huddle around a campfire with you, I can't pull you up a chair next to the fireplace of a rustic country inn and I can't sit under a cherry tree and tell stories as the blossoms fall around us, so I'll have to settle for print and paper. Enjoy.

The Curse of Lycaon

The legend of evil king Lycaon, and his transformation into a wolf-man by Zeus as punishment for cannibalism and blasphemy, was already ancient when the first-century Roman poet Ovid set it down in his book of myths, Metamorphoses. *It is one of the oldest werewolf stories in the world, and a fitting start to this book.*

Clutching his long spear and huddling against the chill gusts that blew through the wooded hills, the palace sentry stood his lonely watch. The sounds of wild feasting drifted out of the palace, carried on the autumn wind—drunken laughter mixed with the shattering of pottery, shouts and curses, the weird tones of foreign music, the clash and clatter of weapons, the terrified screams. The screams were always followed by louder, longer laughter.

The sentry turned away with a look of disgust. Why bother guarding the stronghold of Lycaon, he wondered as he looked out over the landscape under the silver light of the full moon. Who in their right mind would *want* to enter that stinking den of evil? What thief would risk a horrible death—or, perhaps, a fate worse than death—at the hands of the warlord and his cult in order to raid their bloodstained treasury? The terror Lycaon had spread protected his fortress better than an army could have.

It wasn't always so, the soldier thought. There were wars, of course, and killing. One noble lord sending men against another, to die over a scrap of land or an imagined insult. There was drunkenness too, and every kind of offence and vice . But never had anyone sinned against the gods and man like the warlord Lycaon, never had anyone left such a trail of corruption and blasphemy.

He had been a common bandit once, the kind who hides out on the fringes of civilization and takes what he wants from those too weak to keep it for themselves. But soon, through a combination of ruthlessness, cunning and luck, Lycaon's power and fortune grew. Instead of skulking back to his forest hideouts after raids, he began seizing entire settlements, eventually creating for himself a makeshift kingdom in the hills. Evil men joined him by the hundreds, whole armies of thieves and murderers, to share in his plunder.

But robbery and rape were the least of "king" Lycaon's sins, for he was a worshipper of dark and evil forces. At first his devotion to these demons was an act of rebellion, a rejection of the gods of Olympus who were worshipped by the society he hated. But the more his victories mounted, the more he attributed his good fortune to his sinister idols. With every rich town he captured, with every rival who swore allegiance to him or died, his loyalty to these ancient horrors increased. He became a fanatic and brought his amoral followers along with him, until the core of his forces was more cult than army, a band of unholy warriors dedicated to every dark perversion and sacrilege.

Lycaon destroyed shrines and desecrated temples, raising in their place the gaudy altars of his twisted beast-gods. In all the territory he conquered, the proper feasts and observances were thrown out in favor of bizarre rituals. It was at these animalistic orgies that the worst sins were committed: human sacrifice and the eating of human flesh. Hundreds of soldiers, citizens and slaves became foul offerings to Lycaon's demons, and dark delicacies on his table. Through it all, drunk on wine and evil, the depraved bandit king laughed and mocked the gods.

But to resist, to rebel, would be suicide or worse; rulers come and rulers go, and there's nothing for the common people to do but obey and stay faithful to the gods, praying to Zeus for deliverance. Besides, thought the guard with the grim humor of the professional soldier, guard duty wasn't so bad—by keeping people away from Lycaon's fortress of death, he was doing his fellow man a great favor.

The eerie howl of wolves in the hills cut through the noise of the palace orgy and shook the guard out of his morbid daydreaming. There were many wild beasts about these days, lurking unnaturally close to the settlements, and yet their cries in the night never failed to send a shiver down the guard's spine. Turning away from his moonlit view of the wolf-haunted hills, he was surprised to see the figure of an old man coming up the road, shuffling painfully and leaning on a rough wooden staff for support. Why would a graybeard like this be coming to this place, at this time of night? The guard sighed and set the butt of his spear into the dust of the trail, preparing to turn the obviously confused old buzzard away.

"Halt!" he called out when the bent and limping figure came near. "Go back where you came from, grandfather. You've taken the wrong path!"

"Eh?" The old man looked up from the road, gazing at the soldier with keen, clear eyes that seemed out of place in his ancient, white-bearded face. He glanced back down the way he'd come, then up at the stars, before turning back to the sentry. "The wrong road, you say? Are you absolutely certain? I was sure this was the path to the palace of Lycaon, who claims himself king around here."

"Then you weren't mistaken," answered the guard with a slight chuckle, "but you're definitely crazy. The court of Lycaon isn't a place where men with sound minds would go of their own free choice. Begone, and thank me for saving your life!"

With a creak and pop of arthritic joints, the old man drew himself up to as much of his full height as he could muster and glared at the smiling guard. "Ah, but you see, I *do* have business with king Lycaon! A man such as yourself wouldn't recognize my name if I gave it to you, no, but I assure you that my reputation for wisdom opens palace gates around the world! I have traveled a very long way to bring my message to your master, a message he dearly needs to hear. And look at me; I'm a broken-down old man! What possible threat could I be to the king and his court? Now stand aside!"

The guard smiled and held up his hand. "Calm down, grandfather," he said gently. "It's not the king's safety I'm worried about, it's yours. The gods teach us to honor and respect elders such as yourself, and it would be a sin for me to allow you to walk to your death. Listen to them in there! They'd tear you apart for sport!"

The old man leaned past the guard and peered intently at the brightly lit palace. "That bad, eh? Well, the gods will certainly bless you for your faithfulness, young man, but I'm afraid I truly must insist." He gazed up at the guard with his piercing eyes and spoke in a calm voice filled with authority. "Stand aside, and let me pass."

The soldier held the old man's gaze for a moment, then sighed and looked back at Lycaon's deadly house of blasphemy. If this geezer was set on having a nice chat with the king, he thought, what could he do about it? He'd done his duty. The guard lowered his spear and stepped to the side, watching the hunched figure shuffle toward the palace. "May the gods be merciful, grandfather," he muttered.

"Merciful?" the old man called back over his shoulder. "That very much remains to be seen." With that, he disappeared through the brightly lit portal of king Lycaon's notorious feasting-hall.

The scene that greeted the old man when he entered that place was like something out of a nightmare. The enormous hall, grotesquely lit in fiery colors by dozens of huge oil lamps and smoking braziers, held dozens of Lycaon's most favored minions and henchmen, sprawled drunkenly on cushions and couches, attended to by scores of terrified slaves. In every corner of that cursed hall was to be found every vice under the sun and moon, every sin that could be committed by a those with no fear of the wrath of heaven or the justice of men. And over it all stood the hideous crude idols of Lycaon's foul beast-gods, presiding over their servant's depraved court with unblinking gold-gilt eyes.

Amid the noise and smoke and stench, the old man heard screams of unlucky slaves and the flatulent laughter of Lycaon's thugs and courtiers, the insane drones and squeals of the drug-crazed musicians. He stood at the threshold to the hall, silent and watching, his glaring eyes taking in the entire blasphemous scene. At last one of the men, looking up from the serving-girl he had been occupied with, noticed the robed figure in the doorway and whistled sharply for attention.

The hush that suddenly fell over that hellish hall was almost complete, broken only by the semiconscious moans and sobs of those slaves and prisoners that had been tormented. Still the old man stood, staring with cold fire at the gathered disciples of Lycaon's cult, not speaking but seeming to send out waves of righteous rage. The feast-goers, who a second ago were filled with boasting arrogance, suddenly found themselves speechless and intimidated, like misbehaving schoolboys who've been caught by their teacher.

At last one of Lycaon's court, braver or more drunken than the others, spoke up to break the building tension. "Grandfather!" he called in a mocking tone. "Grandfather, you've come! Look, everyone, our grandfather has come to join our little party!" There was a round of relieved laughter, and another henchman got into the spirit of his companion's cruel game. "Yes," this other one laughed, "it's grandfather's birthday party, didn't you know? He's 200 years old today!" More boozy laughter followed, and more shallow jeers and catcalls.

"Well, honored grandfather," said the man who'd first spoken, with an evil grin and eyes like a hungry jackal, "to what do we owe the pleasure of this visit? Did you get lost on the way to the latrine again?"

"I came," said the old man in deadly cold tones, "because I had heard a great many interesting stories about your master, and I wished to speak with him. Where is he? Where is 'king' Lycaon?"

"King Lycaon is here, grandfather," a wine-sodden but deep and powerful voice boomed out across the room. On a raised platform at one end of the feasting-hall, below the largest of the obscene gold-covered idols, a mighty figure rose up from a nest of embroidered cushions, rich cloths and fawning slave girls. In a rich robe of wolf fur, his feet bare and his fingers heavy with gold rings, Lycaon stood. Powerfully built and heavily bearded, fat with feasting and flushed with wine, the bandit-lord looked for all the world like one of the hall's bestial demon-idols brought to life. Amid the decadence of his silks and servants, he glared darkly down the length of the hall at the old man who stood under the great arch of the doorway.

"King Lycaon is here," he repeated, "and he wonders why his feast has been interrupted by an uninvited guest. Although he is curious about which 'stories' may have been spread that attracted the attention of such an honored old boot such as yourself." With a joyless, toothy grin he drained his heavy wine goblet and let it fall to the floor; the ring and clatter of metal on stone was deafening in the silent hall.

"The story is told, O king," replied the old man, "that Lycaon alone was brave enough to cast out and banish the gods of Olympus from his tiny kingdom, and that he has replaced them with dark idols. I have also heard that in his worship of these demons he has committed unspeakable crimes and atrocities."

"Unspeakable?" Lycaon roared with drunken amusement, a bellow of laughter like a rumble of thunder. "You ancient piece of vulture-bait, didn't you hear the rest of the story? There are no 'unspeakable' acts in Lycaon's kingdom! Here, we are free to do and say what we please. So go ahead and 'speak' these crimes. Torture, rape, murder, blasphemy? Yes, yes and yes! All this and more has Lycaon done in the name of his masters, and more still will he do on his path to power!"

The old man's voice nearly broke with rage, but remained level as he replied. "I see. So you freely admit to these crimes against the laws of the gods?"

"Admit? No, Lycaon *admits* nothing...he revels in it! Why shouldn't he? His gods are the gods of pleasure and riches, of power and dominion over men. Since he has served them, they have smiled upon him and granted him victory in battle, a kingdom to rule and wealth beyond the dreams of a skulking bandit in the woods. But they demand sacrifice, grandfather, and hate the weak laws of the old gods and their cowering worshippers. And so Lycaon kills in their name, and takes what he wants, and gives his masters their sacrifices, and he will continue to do so, and continue to be blessed, until the whole world trembles at his feet!"

"*Enough!*" The old man's shout blasted through the room, far beyond the capacity of an elderly voice. Before the eyes of the astonished court of Lycaon, the bent and gray-haired wanderer began to change, even as he spoke.

"You have sinned greatly, all of you," he thundered, as his gnarled back straightened and he stood tall. "You have cast out the gods of your fathers and replaced them with false gods and idols!" His ragged white beard grew full and dark, as black hair began to sprout to cover his once-bald head. "You have broken every vow and perverted everything good and natural!" The dust of travel fell from his grimy robes, leaving cloth of pure white covering a powerful warrior's frame. "I am Zeus, your god, and you *will* beg for mercy!"

The power of command radiated out from the regal figure on the threshold of the hall, standing where a second ago there had been only a laughable old hermit. With all the glamor of their idolatrous orgy stripped away, the gathered disciples of bloodthirsty Lycaon fell to their knees; there was truly a god in the room now, rather than a collection of mere wooden monstrosities, and all those craven villains suddenly found their old faith and rushed to beg forgiveness. All, that is, except one.

"Fools!" roared Lycaon. The king was sunk so deep in his demon-worship that even the presence of Zeus himself failed to move him. "Sniveling fools! Get on your feet! Can't you see it's a trick? The old man and this muscle-bound actor have dazzled you with cheap stage gimmicks! Get up, Lycaon orders you!"

The force of Lycaon's command caused some of the kneeling thugs to raise their heads, confused and doubting. What if it *was* a trick? They knew what Lycaon would do, in his idols' names, to those who disobeyed.

But none rose, so in awe were they of the figure in the doorway.

Seeing that none of his former minions were obeying his commands, the crafty Lycaon came up with a different tactic. All he needed to do, he reasoned, was *prove* to these cowards that this stranger was human rather than divine. Luckily, there was an easy test close at hand—a serving platter of roast human leg-meat. A mortal could be fooled into eating this delicacy, but a god could not. One little bite, thought Lycaon in his drunk and evil brain, and this big bruiser would be next on the roasting-spit.

"Very well," said Lycaon, abruptly changing his tone. "Let Lycaon be the first to welcome and serve our honored guest!" Picking up the gold-wrought platter from the low table on his royal platform, Lycaon marched unsteadily to the entryway to the hall, where the huge man waited with eyes like glowing coals. Kneeling before the stranger, Lycaon offered up the platter of cursed meat.

"The finest suckling pig, O mighty Zeus," declared Lycaon, smiling to himself as he bowed his head low. "Please, take Lycaon's hospitality and refresh yourself."

All eyes in the hall were fixed on the two figures in the doorway, the kneeling king of bandits and the towering figure of the once-old man who named himself as king of the gods. All knew what was on the platter, and all waited to see what would become of this terrible encounter. Seconds dragged by like hours as the whole of the universe seemed to turn upon that single spot.

"Stand up," said the stranger at last, in a deadly quiet voice that was, if anything, more powerful than his shout. Proud Lycaon found himself compelled to obey, unable to resist, and stood facing the stranger with the golden tray still clutched in his hands, white-knuckled and trembling. Power filled the room as a low rumbling was heard and the earth itself seemed to tremble.

"No man would dare what you have dared," the stranger continued in that same quiet voice, every word ringing clear despite the growing rumble in the great hall. "But you are not a man, are you, 'king' Lycaon? You are a beast, a beast that somehow found itself wearing the wrong shape. I will correct that error now." With that, the stranger reached out and touched the robber-lord's sweating brow.

The tray, with its unclean cargo, clattered to the floor. Lycaon found himself suddenly filled with the deepest fear; it was a soul-eating body terror, consuming every fiber of his being and filling him with one desire: to flee. The greasy fires that warmed and lit the grand feast-hall terrified him, as did the pale faces of his once-loyal followers. Even the mere fact of being inside, surrounded by walls and covered over with a roof, brought him to the point of mindless panic. He had to get out, get outside, get *away*. And, as the sudden earthquake grew stronger and the forbidden idols began to crack and topple, that's exactly what he did.

Lycaon ran out into the night, into the woods and hills, running on instinct away from the lights and fires of human society that now so terrified him. As he ran and his first panic subsided, he tried to call out to his evil gods, the demons who he thought had protected him and made him a king, but no words would come out. All he could do was howl and whine like a beast. In horror, he looked

down at his hands and watched as they grew longer and were covered with coarse hair, the nails hardening and hooking into claws.

Lycaon's body was wracked with pain, and he began to writhe on the ground in agony. His legs cracked and splintered, the bones resetting themselves so that his legs bent like those of a dog. Burning with fever, he tried to rip his rich cloak away, only to find that he was ripping his own flesh—the luxurious wolf fur was now part of his body, covering him head to toe. But his mind was still the mind of a man, and he was conscious of the doom that had been brought down on him.

Forever would he be cursed to walk the earth on the fringes of society, one of the creatures of the night and the forest, skulking in the shadows and scavenging a living, existing for eternity as a warning from the gods to those who would abandon justice and humanity and make themselves into beasts.

The bitter tears of a man streamed down his furry muzzle as he looked down through the trees. With night-seeing animal eyes he watched as his gilded feasting-hall collapsed and was consumed by cleansing flame. And there in the woods, under the mocking light of the full moon, Lycaon the former robber-king howled his rage and regret.

Far off, across the hills, his cry was answered by a pack of wolves calling to their lost brother, while down below a puzzled sentry watched his hated master's palace burn to the ground. He gave a silent prayer of thanks to the justice of the gods.

The Wolf-Man

The following story is based on a story recorded by George Bird Grinnell in Blackfoot Lodge Tales, *published in 1892. Grinnell, a writer, explorer, ethnologist and founder of what would become Glacier National Park in Montana, was one of the few European men of his time with any interest in or ability to understand the cultures of Native people.* Blackfoot Lodge Tales, *researched and collected only a few years after the disappearance of the buffalo destroyed a way of life, remains an invaluable record of Blackfoot spirituality and society.*

I selected "The Wolf-Man" for adaptation for a number of reasons. First, the shape-changing hero is a normal man, rather than a legendary warrior or trickster god, as is more usual. Second, it not only illustrates the Native connection to the animal and spirit worlds, but contains many universal themes common to shapeshifting legends around the world: transformation as a return from death or near-death; transformation as a result of betrayal; and transformation as revenge for a crime against nature.

Third, and maybe most important, it's simply a cool story.

The huge skull shone in the sunset light, buffalo bone on the crest of the ridge, bleached by years of prairie sun, wind and rain. It was One Arrow's favorite lookout point, a lonely landmark on the vast land, and as the Blackfoot hunter strode toward the familiar skull, the sigh of the wind masked the nearly silent rustle of his footsteps through the grass. From that point he could see for miles, track the movements of the buffalo and keep watch for any approaching enemies brave or crazy enough to come raiding in his people's territory.

Reaching the ridgetop, One Arrow stretched and sat down on the massive headbone, his customary seat during his daily lookout. Resting his spear across his knees, he slowly scanned the land spread out before him. All quiet, as usual, apart from a few scattered buffalo grazing a ways off to the east. And far to the south, just on the long line of the horizon, he could see—or imagined he could see— the smudge of smoke that would mark the camp of his people, the place of friends and family he'd withdrawn from many long days ago.

Ah, so far away, the hunter thought sadly, longing for the lodges where even now men would be calling out feasts, sharing good food and good stories and passing the pipe. His self-imposed seclusion went against his friendly nature, and was frowned upon in the traditions of his people, but to his thinking he'd had no other choice. Those two wicked wives of his had been causing him more embarrassment with every passing day, their shameless behavior making him a laughingstock and worse in the eyes of his brothers. In the end, withdrawal from society in the hope he could teach those two to be good had been his only choice.

Each had been a sweet-seeming girl, well brought-up in a good family, and he'd taken them as wives almost at the same time. But once he'd established his household with them, something changed. He was a good provider, but they became greedy even as they became lazy, wheedling him for luxuries and trinkets, constantly comparing him loudly with any other man who happened to be more successful at the time. His older first wife had become a bully, with his younger wife as her cowed underling. They would gossip, flirt shamelessly and cause trouble; it seemed, in fact, that they could do nothing without causing trouble.

One Arrow was a good hunter and warrior—he'd earned his name through his deadly accuracy with his bow—but his lodge had become shabby, his property sunk into disarray, his good name brought down. Of course, he could have easily divorced them; it was a simple matter of sending them back to their relations and demanding the bride-price he'd paid. But a man needs wives and he had no others, and with his household in such a state it would be difficult if not impossible to win another bride. Most of all, though, he was a kind-hearted man—many of his relations were of the opinion that his soft hand with his wives had spoiled them—and he remembered the good girls he'd thought they'd been. He didn't want to see the two women subjected to the shame and punishments they'd receive if he sent them away from his lodge. So, with the women alternately crying and cursing, he'd moved his lodge and household far out onto the prairie—far from society, far enough that he could hunt alone without driving away the game his people needed to survive—in the hope that he could teach his bad wives to be good.

It's been many days, and I've been firm with them, he thought, looking out across the land daubed in red and gold by the setting sun. Taking his feathered spear in hand once more, he gathered his lean body up from his buffalo-skull chair and turned back toward the lonesome campsite where his troublesome women waited.

Maybe tonight, he added wearily as he began his walk back down the grassy ridge, *they'll actually have something ready for me to eat.*

Shading her eyes, One Arrow's first wife looked away toward the ridge where her husband, a speck in the distance, sat with his back to their camp. With a snort of disgust she turned to the younger woman who sat behind her, half-heartedly doing some beadwork.

"Every day, he sits up there on that nasty old skull," the older woman said with a snarl, "staring off into space while we wait down here with nothing to do but his household chores. There's nobody to talk to, no feasts, no nice things, not even any buffalo—just rabbits and deer and dirt and *him.*"

She snorted again. "He's going to expect something to eat when he's finished ignoring us too; drop that beadwork and start preparing some food."

The second wife did as she was told, literally dropping the beadwork and moving angrily to begin cooking some meat. "I wouldn't mind cooking," she said, pouting, "if there was somebody besides him and you to share it with. Remember the feasts we used to have? Now there's nobody. We're so far away, even if we walked all day, we wouldn't meet another person. I'm tired of living apart from people!"

"I'm tired of it too." One Arrow's first wife got a crafty look in her eye. "And I've been thinking about what we can do about it."

"What we can do about it?" The younger woman laughed bitterly. "What do you mean 'what we can do about it?' We can't do *anything* about it. We're his wives, and he won't divorce us, and we can't just walk back to our fathers' lodges. No, we're stuck tanning rabbit skins in the middle of nowhere until *he* decides we've learned our lesson!" With this last statement, she shook her finger and dropped her voice in imitation of her husband's.

The older wife laughed. "Well, I don't like this lesson, and I have an idea of what we can do to end it ourselves. It's true we're far away from all our friends and relations; we can't talk to them, they can't hear us call. But *he* can't talk to them either, and they can't hear him call. There's nobody around to know anything that goes on in this camp."

The younger woman sat, silent and staring, as she began to realize what the other was saying. One Arrow's first wife continued in a wicked, low voice. "I say, let's kill our husband. We'll say he disappeared out hunting, and return to our relations and have a good time."

"But how do we kill him?" the second wife replied. "He's a good fighter; if we try to stab him or club him and don't kill him right away, we're done for."

"Ah! As usual, I've thought of everything, Little Sister," the older wife teased. "But look; our husband will be back soon." She pointed up at the ridge where One Arrow could be seen getting up from his customary perch, standing and stretching. "Finish cooking that meat and I'll tell you my plan."

The next day dawned cold, the air carrying with it the feel of winter. One Arrow awoke early, but his two wives were already up, bustling about and getting his clothes and equipment ready for hunting. The exasperated man was pleasantly surprised—those two usually needed to be all but dragged out of bed in the morning. Yawning and rising from his warm blankets and furs, One Arrow left his lodge to prepare for the hunt.

"Good morning, husband!" his first wife called out cheerfully from where she sat arranging his arrows and checking his bow and spear. "Good morning!" his second wife echoed, looking up from the pouch she was filling with pemmican, the dried meat mixed with berries and buffalo fat that would be One Arrow's meal on the hunting trail.

"Good morning," he answered, gladdened by the hope that maybe these two women were finally coming back around to better habits; they were behaving, he thought, like newlywed brides. "I must say, this is a surprise; I'm not used to seeing you two up and busy so early in the day. Are you sure you are my wives? Maybe a spirit has come and possessed my wives' bodies!"

"Don't tease us!" said the younger woman, making an exaggerated pout. "We just want to get you started on your hunt quickly. First wife had a very strong dream last night."

"Is that so?" asked the amused hunter, turning to his older bride. "And what was this dream you had?"

One Arrow's first wife turned and scowled at the other woman; One Arrow even imagined he saw his shameless wife blush. "You weren't supposed to say anything!" she hissed. Turning back to her husband with her head tilted proudly and her eyes defiant, she continued, "But yes, laugh at me if you want, but I did have a powerful dream.

A wolf-spirit appeared to me and told me that in this day's hunting, my husband was to set out as early as possible, and to stay out for at least two days. I know it is a true dream!"

The lean hunter laughed, but kindly. "What now? My first wife is a prophet? I suppose I was luckier in marriage than I thought!" Seeing the angry fires begin sparking in her eyes, he softened his teasing. "But you speak well; this might really be a powerful dream. It makes good sense, anyway; the farther off I hunt, the less chance I'll have of angering the *I-kun-uh'-kah-tsi*, the Society of All Comrades that administers justice. Already, people are unhappy at my withdrawal from society; if they thought I was ruining their hunting, they'd punish me for sure. So I'll follow your advice and move farther away to hunt."

"Oh, thank you!" she cried, not having to pretend her excitement; her plan was working perfectly. "Here's your bow and spear, and here are your arrows. There's enough pemmican in here for three days, at least. You should hurry and get started."

"All right, all right," One Arrow laughed again. "I'm going! Did your wolf-spirit say I have to run all the way too?" He playfully shook the string of wolf's teeth and wooden beads he'd worn around his neck since his first war journey as a young man. Taking his food and equipment, he waved goodbye and headed out across the miles of windswept grassland.

For a long time his first wife watched him go, her eyes hard with hate, until at last he was the smallest of dots, the long grass and gently rolling prairie hiding him from view. Her eyes still focused on One Arrow's vanishing point, she spoke over her shoulder to her subordinate.

"I really did have a dream last night, a powerful dream," she said in a thoughtful tone. "A wolf dream even! I dreamed a powerful wolf, a big gray hunter, fell into a deadfall marked by an old buffalo skull. He was injured, and he howled to call his brothers, but he couldn't escape from the pit."

"If that's so, I think it's a good sign," replied the younger woman. "It means our plan—your plan—can't fail, I think. What happened next in the dream?"

"Ah, that I don't know; I woke up just then," the first wife said, returning to her usual bossy tone. "But," she added, "I woke up smiling. Now hurry up and grab the things we need. We've got a wolf-trap to dig!"

Digging a hole is a hot and heavy job, and those two—though the second wife got the worst of it, of course—did more hard work in one day up on the ridge than they'd probably done in their lives. Sweating and cursing, dusty and dry, they dug through turf and soil, dirt and sand, all through that day and the next morning. Two feet, four feet, six feet down they made their hole, finally covering it up expertly with light brush and grass. It was an excellent deadfall, the kind the men used to capture predators that couldn't be herded or hunted.

Picking up the big old skull, the first wife gingerly placed it on the verge of the pit they'd dug, at the edge farthest from their camp. The enormous headbone stared blankly across the prairie. "There! Now when he comes up here to sit, he'll walk across our trap and that'll be it for him," she said with a chuckle. "We'll soon be free to end this ridiculous isolation and return to our friends and relations." With one last check to make sure the hole was as invisible as could be, she led her exhausted fellow wife back to their lodge.

The campsite was, of course, a mess; for nearly two days the two women had done nothing but dig their pit up on the ridge, returning only to eat and rest, and the place was littered with bones and scraps and unfinished work. The younger woman, forgetting for a moment the deadly work they'd just completed, sighed in dismay. "Now I suppose we'll have to get this camp in order."

The elder wife just looked at her with an amused expression, a smile that didn't reach her hard eyes.

"Why should we?" she asked, laughing coldly.

One Arrow returned to his lodge slowly, loaded down with as much deer meat as he could carry; it had been a good hunt and he was happy, singing an old trail song to himself in the late afternoon sun as he neared the camp. But when he approached and saw the state of things, and his two wives just sitting doing nothing, his good mood disappeared like smoke.

"Hey, you two! What's the matter with you? I go out hunting for less than two days, and I come back to find you haven't done any work at all. Look," he said, kicking at an unfinished piece of embroidery that lay on the ground, "this is exactly where it was two days ago. And look at yourselves; you're covered in dust and dirt. When I left, I'd thought you might be coming around...what've you been doing?"

His first wife got to her feet and hurried to her angry husband, speaking in very apologetic tones. "I'm sorry, I'm sorry; while you were gone, we began to quarrel over who was to do what, and neither of us would yield to the other so nothing got done. We even ended up fighting, rolling on the ground like wrestlers, and that's why you find us so dirty."

"Fighting with each other, rolling on the ground like children?" One Arrow couldn't believe what he was hearing, and his long frustration began to show as he raised his voice. "What's gotten into you? What am I supposed to do with two wives like you? Should I beat you? Should I divorce you? What? Tell me, what?"

"Please, husband, we're sorry," the woman said soothingly. "We were foolish when you were gone, but now you're back and we're sorry. Please, just leave that good meat you've brought and we'll cook some for you while you go up to your lookout on the ridge. You can punish us if you want, after you've rested and eaten."

Looking from his first wife's pleading face to his younger bride, who still sat staring up at him, all One Arrow wanted was to be back out on the hunting trail, alone and happy and away from these two. His plan to reform them hadn't worked; he didn't know what else to do. Angry and despairing at what his situation had come to, he spun away without a word and stormed through the long grass toward his place of seclusion.

His first wife watched him go, wringing her hands, and her younger conspirator bit down on a knuckle. Neither moved, neither spoke; it was as if everything in the world had stopped except the figure of One Arrow walking up that hill. Their hearts beat faster, they could barely breathe as he got closer and closer to the top of the ridge. It seemed to take forever, the minutes dragging past until finally their unsuspecting husband took that single, fateful step and...

...vanished. Dropped out of sight as though he'd never been there, swallowed by the earth. The waiting women heard one loud cry, and then came silence. There was no sound to be heard beyond the thunder of their pulse in their ears and the ghostly rush of wind over the land, and no movement to be seen up on the ridge.

"It worked," the younger woman whispered at last. "It worked. Our husband is dead!"

For One Arrow, it became an eternity of dreamless nothing. It could have been a moment that passed, it could have been days, it could have been a thousand years; in that limbo there was no telling, no caring. The first glimmers of returning consciousness, when they came, knew only the timelessness, the peace, the dark. *So this is death*, thought One Arrow peacefully, floating. *I wonder what happens next?*

Endless time drifted by, until One Arrow thought he could hear a rushing sound surrounding him, a noise increasing in volume until it became a dull roar. Along with the sound came a feeling of coldness, a deep chill that filled every part of him and masked the ache in his body. *Body?* thought One Arrow, puzzled. *It seems odd that I should be feeling the hurts of my body after death. Unless, of course, I'm not really dead...*

Full consciousness crashed down upon him then, in a wave of pain and realization, and the trapped man woke to a world of misery. He remembered walking up the hill, remembered the yielding feel of his first angry step onto the fragile surface of the deadfall, remembered the sudden plunge into total darkness. He was in darkness still, but this was the honest, natural dark of night; from where he lay, he could see the circle of the night sky in the mouth of the pit above him, his groggy vision causing the stars to waver and swim as if they were stars reflected in a pool of water. He was very cold, and every ragged breath sent a spearpoint of fire through his chest.

Broken rib, One Arrow thought with a sense of detachment, *maybe more than one.* That wasn't too bad; he'd broken a rib or two before. As he lay shivering in the bottom of the pit and became more aware of his body, he thought he felt a solid weight lying on top of him, pinning his left arm. Cautiously, he tried moving his right arm. There was no pain that he could feel, so he reached over to feel what it was that he lay under. His fingers found the familiar texture of weathered bone, and One Arrow almost laughed out loud. *Well, Brother Buffalo*, he thought with bitterness, *it looks like those two have trapped us both. And now it's you that sits on me!*

He knew exactly what had happened; he'd known as soon as the ground had given way beneath his feet. His wicked wives had finally dared to go beyond complaints and insults and evil looks, had dared the unthinkable. There was no one else who could have dug this pit, and no one to hear him should he waste his breath calling for help—no one but the murderous women who had put him there in the first place. If he was going to live to see justice done, he'd have to handle his own rescue.

Shivering and weak, but fuelled by rage and resolve, One Arrow tried to raise himself up.

A white explosion of agony tore through his body, and he momentarily blacked out once more. Coming to in a red haze of shock and pain, sweating and gasping for breath, One Arrow realized his injuries were far worse than a couple broken ribs and a knock on the head. His right leg was fractured. Though the rim of the pit couldn't be more than six feet above where he lay, it might as well have been on the moon if he couldn't stand up to reach it. He thought about twisting himself to get his uninjured left leg underneath him, but even a slight twitch brought a new blast of pain and a shower of sparks before his eyes, forcing him to beat back unconsciousness.

Panting and delirious, One Arrow fell back and laid still. He was terribly thirsty; how long had he lain in the pit? There was no way he could tell. Without water, without help, there was no way he could survive the trap he wives had left for him, so he prepared himself for the arrival of death. Looking up at the sky, he found himself thinking about the trap he was in, exactly the kind of trap his people sometimes used to catch animals, like wolves, that were too quick or too elusive to stalk with a bow. It was excellently made, he had to admit, and the thought struck his fading mind as being quite funny. He laughed out loud then, a dry, painful chuckle through his parched throat.

"Well...what do you think of that, brother?" he whispered to the bleached skull that still rested on his chest. "So much time spent...trying to make my wives into good housekeepers...when all along they were natural hunters!"

One Arrow's last gasp of laughter trailed off into a fit of coughing, but he was quickly moving beyond feeling the pain the spasm caused in his chest. The little circle of bright stars above him began to fade as his sight dimmed and his eyes closed. He was leaving the world again, and as he slipped away the vision of his eyes was replaced with the vision of his soul—a gray wolf, trapped, calling out for his brothers.

A powerful dream, the dying man thought as the blackness closed over him once more.

Loping easily through the long grass, He-Howls-First thought it was a particularly fine night to be a wolf. Clear skies with plenty of starshine and a fang-like sliver of moon provided perfect light for hunting. The hissing of the breeze ruffling his fur was strong enough to mask the sound of his passage, but not so strong as to disturb and tangle the wonderful web of smells that surrounded him—the sweet grass, the cool scent of a creek, the earthy aroma of a group of buffalo over the next rise. And what was this other smell? Men?

How interesting, the wandering hunter thought, pausing and sniffing the air to better decipher the scent. A very small camp, he deduced, no more than three or four two-legged people, and not much meat; if these humans had been slaughtering buffalo, there might have been plenty of delicious morsels for the taking. But what were these people doing so far from their pack? He-Howls-First's curiosity was piqued, and he stalked forward toward the smell of tanned hides and campfire ashes, the smell of human beings.

Approaching, he realized the campsite had been vacated not long before, probably earlier that very evening. The human-scent was still strong around the place, the ashes in the pit still giving off the smell of smoldering brush and buffalo chips. The hungry wolf counted himself lucky to have come across such a freshly broken camp, and hurried down toward the site to grab the ready scraps and good marrow-bones men leave behind. His mind on his midnight snack, He-Howls-First was almost to the place where the lodge had stood before he caught a troubling new scent carried on the wind blowing down from a nearby ridge. It was the mingled smell of man, fear and death.

This just gets more and more strange, the wolf thought as he cautiously trotted up the ridge. *A quickly abandoned camp in the middle of nowhere, and now a dying man. What's going on here?* He'd been the inquisitive type ever since he was a pup, and a mystery this exciting didn't often come along in the unchanging life of the plains. The blood smell grew stronger as he mounted the rise, and he tracked it to its unexpected source—a wolf-trap dug into the summit of the hill.

Peering down into the pit, He-Howls-First saw the crumpled form of a man lying at the bottom. The man smelled almost like dead meat, and there was a great amount of blood spilled. But the sensitive wolf could detect the life that remained in the man, could feel the heat still coming off his body and hear the faint whisper of his fading breath. It was all very puzzling—what was a man doing lying in a wolf-trap, so far from his fellow men? The confused wolf had to take some time to think hard about this problem and what to do about it. At last he came up with what he thought was a brilliant plan, and raised his shaggy head to call his fellow wolves.

"*A-hooo-ooo!* Come and see what I've found! *A-hooo-oooo!*"

His call went out across the starlit prairie, and was soon answered by several of his kind. The clever wolf waited patiently by the pit for his brothers to arrive. He didn't wait long; He-Howls-First had a good reputation for finding interesting and useful things—and easy meals. Soon there were a number of curious wolves gathered on the ridge, as well as a number of coyotes, kit-foxes and badgers; where wolves went, so went their smaller brothers looking for leftovers. All these animals crowded around He-Howls-First and his hole in the ground, sniffing the strange smell of the dying man and wondering what it could all mean.

When he had a good-sized audience, He-Howls-First spoke up. "Here in this hole is my find, brothers," he said, proudly. "Here is a fallen-in man." There was a murmur of curious growls and yips from the gathered canines. "It is my idea," the wolf continued, "that we dig him out from this pit, and take him as our brother." The murmur grew louder as the amazed wild dogs began to debate the situation with each other.

A bold coyote who had been leaning far over the edge of the trap to better sniff the fallen man pulled his head out of the hole to reply. "Ah, but he's nearly dead," he whined. "He already smells more like carrion than a living man. Soon he'll be good dead meat." The hungry scavenger licked his chops at the thought, and poked his muzzle back into the hole as a few of his brothers barked in agreement.

"I hear you, and you speak well," He-Howls-First replied, "but please listen to my idea, and see if you can follow my thinking." He waited for the barks and whines to die down before continuing. "Here is a man, fallen into a wolf-trap. Who digs wolf-traps? The buffalo? The crows? No; only men dig traps, and they remember where they've dug so they don't fall into them themselves. So this man has fallen into a trap prepared for him by other men. Do you see where the camp was, down below? That lodge did not walk away by itself. This man was left to die by other men; to the world of men, he is dead."

He-Howls-First paused to let that sink in, and the noise of the animals' discussion grew again. "But!" he barked at last, "we know he is alive, if only barely. We could rescue him, dig him out and take him for our brother. Think of how much help a man's medicine could be to us! He knows the ways of men, knows how and when they hunt. He knows tools and knows how men build things; he could help us avoid traps and snares."

"Just like he avoided this one, eh?" squealed a badger from the edge of the little crowd. There was some laughter, but soon the group was seriously debating the matter of what to do with this trapped man who had been cast off by his people. Finally, they came to a decision.

"You speak well, brother," said one of the wolves that were gathered there. "We think your plan is a good one. Let's dig this man out."

With that, they began to dig a tunnel sloping down to the bottom of the trap. The work went quickly—especially with the help of the badgers and kit-foxes, who love to dig although they put on a show of grumbling about it—and soon they had almost reached the man they hoped to have as a brother. When there was only a little dirt left to be moved away, He-Howls-First spoke up again.

"There is one last thing we have to decide," he said, "and that is the issue of who our new brother is to live with. I submit that because it was a wolf who found him, and because he is closest in size to us big wolves, that he should come live with us." The other animals thought this was fine, and said so, and He-Howls-First clawed out the last bit of earth and dragged the bloody and unconscious man up into the fresh air and starlight.

"He needs strength to walk," said the clever wolf to one of his fellows. "Go quickly, and bring back a good fresh kidney while we keep his body warm." The other wolf ran off while the animals all crowded around the dying man. He soon returned with a fresh, dripping kidney. He-Howls-First took it, and let the warm drippings of the juicy meat fall into the man's open mouth.

The half-dead human moaned, causing some of the skittish foxes to yelp and scamper off to a safe distance, to watch through the grass as he began to stir. "Look, every-one!" barked He-Howls-First with glee, as the man's eyes flicked open and struggled to focus. "Our brother's alive!"

The animal musk of wolf-fur. The taste of fresh blood in his mouth. The low growls and whines of an ancient language. Powerful silver shapes moving in the starlight. Yellow eyes over a white-fanged muzzle stained red. *I'm back in the world of the wolf-dream*, thought One Arrow as his mind returned once more from the dreamless, thoughtless dark. A dream world of motion and freedom, power and grace. A world of ancient brotherhood, of the unending cycle of life.

But along with consciousness came the pain of his injuries, the thirst and the chill of shock. The unfortunate Blackfoot soon realized this was no dream. The bloodstained jaws that filled his vision were those of a real wolf, a huge gray beast standing over him, glaring with golden eyes.

One Arrow wasn't afraid; he was beyond fear by now. But he froze under the predator's gaze, locked eyes with the wolf, and the animal reflex inside kept him from slipping back into the dark, kept him away from the edge of unconsciousness. He lay like that for a long time, until the wolf bent his muzzle to the ground and nudged something toward him. The wounded hunter looked down and saw the wet, round mass of a fresh elk kidney.

One Arrow's hunger and thirst came back in full force, and he reached out for the raw organ; survival took precedence over daintiness. He realized now that he hadn't been dreaming the flavor of blood in his mouth, that this wolf had saved him from the darkness by sharing his kill. He didn't understand it, and he didn't then take the time to try as he hungrily tore into the juicy morsel.

Eating, he felt his strength and clarity returning, and as he devoured the kidney he began to take in his surroundings. In the starlight he could see the gaping, ragged-edged pit his scheming wives had dug, and at his feet the smaller tunnel he must have been pulled through when he was rescued.

Rescued? As the warm blood and meat strengthened him and cleared his mind, the circumstances of his rescue began to dawn on him. He realized he was surrounded by a pack of animals like he'd only heard about in stories, a circle of species staring at him in the starlight. There were the coyotes, ears up and alert, with the scrappy badgers at their feet and a number of skittish kit foxes behind them, craning their necks to look at the man lying on the ground. In front of all these were the wolves, led by the shaggy silver beast whose eyes were still locked on his, whose jaws were still red with life-saving blood.

One Arrow should have been terrified, but here, in the middle of a pack of killers and scavengers, he felt as safe as if he'd been in one of the lodges of his own people. Strange as it was, hadn't these wolves saved his life? He raised his head and opened his mouth to say his proper thanks, but the effort made his head spin and he collapsed, exhausted beyond endurance, onto the turf of the ridge.

I'll thank them properly when I wake up, he thought as the spinning stars faded and he tumbled into the warm world of natural sleep.

One Arrow's eyes opened to the half light of...dawn? No. Something wasn't right. The air was too dry, too stale. This glow wasn't coming from a rising sun about to brighten the east; it was the afterglow of a sun that had long since gone to its rest in the west. This was nightfall. A whole day—at least—had passed while he slept.

He came fully awake, pulling himself up onto his elbows, and the motion disturbed the furry shapes that lay on either side of him, the wolves that had kept his recovering body warm. Wolf heads turned, regarding him with wolf eyes, and still he felt no fear, only brotherhood and gratitude. There were no more thoughts of this being some kind of dream. The crowd of animals from before had mostly dispersed; only a few wolves and a couple curious coyotes, ranged around him in a small semicircle, remained to welcome him back from sleep.

He was still weak, dazed, thirsty, aching—but One Arrow had never felt so secure, so confident. He felt the ancient kinship between these animals, powerful currents that now flowed to include him, and a kind of primal joy filled his heart. He'd been reborn, he thought; he'd never again be the man he was.

A sudden sharp twinge in his leg, part crackling pain and part burning itch, reminded him: he was still a man, and a badly injured man at that. He looked down at his fractured limb and saw it coated in what looked like a mixture of mud, blood, grasses, leaves and half-chewed bannock. One Arrow went to scrape the mess off in order to examine his wounds—and maybe scratch the itch—but his hand was intercepted by an insistent muzzle, and a low growl kept him from pressing the issue. *It must be wolf-medicine*, he thought, his body and mind beginning to find pleasure in the tingling cold fire of the earthy mixture that covered his leg from ankle to knee.

"Thank you, brothers," he said aloud, and a half-dozen pairs of canine ears pricked up.

The big gray wolf, the one One Arrow knew to be his patron in this strange company, came trotting up with another large piece of fresh meat and stood by while the wounded man hungrily ate his fill. *I could get to like this,*

One Arrow thought as he licked the blood from his fingers. When he'd finished, the wolf came up close beside him on his right and put his shaggy head under the man's hand, arching his back. One Arrow got the message; slowly, carefully, leaning heavily on the wolf's powerful shoulders, he pulled himself up to his feet.

The expected blast of pain from his cracked legbone never came. The strange herbal plaster of wolf-medicine took the edge off the agony and reduced it to a level a man could tolerate. The gray wolf stood fully as tall as One Arrow's waist, making a perfect living crutch for the wounded hunter. Once he was relatively steady on his feet, his fingers curled in the wolf's coarse fur, his guide began walking, leading the limping man slowly across the starlit grasslands with a guard of wolves around him.

One Arrow was surprised at how well he was managing with his wounded leg, and wondered at the hidden secrets of the wolves' medicine. He felt so good, in fact, that when he heard the first trickling sounds of a stream he and his companions were approaching, it was only the steady presence of the big wolf at his side that kept him from trying to trot faster than even the powerful salve would allow. He was terribly thirsty, and when he at last pitched himself flat on the cool pebbled shore of the creek—his injury wouldn't allow him to kneel—he drank as if he was gulping from the last river in the world.

Once he'd quenched his thirst, the strange procession resumed their walk across the prairie. One Arrow didn't know where he was being led, and had a difficult time keeping his bearings as he walked. This worried him a little. He'd prided himself on his sense of direction, but here he couldn't keep things clear in his mind. It felt like they were walking a straight path, but the stars seemed to wheel and shift position, and landmarks in the distance would disappear by the time the travelers got to where they should have been. Still, he trusted his new friends, his rescuers, and let them lead him into their strange territory.

After walking for what seemed like several hours but must have been less—there was still no hint of pre-dawn in the east—a few of the wolves that had been traveling with him ran on ahead, and soon One Arrow and his tireless supporter were approaching a large cave-mouth cut into the side of a sandy bluff. On the packed earth in front of this entryway were gathered a large number of wolves, adult males and females as well as a few pups and adolescent wolves that peered out with wide eyes from behind their elders' shoulders. There were some curious yips and barks, but for the most part everything was silent as rescuer and rescued walked into the dark tunnel.

The darkness of the cave reminded the man of the darkness of his wives' trap, and the darkness of unconsciousness. Already it seemed to him that that was something from the distant past, another lifetime. *Can it really have been only two or three days?* he wondered as he allowed himself to be led deeper into the rough passage. The tunnel was high enough that he could walk more or less upright, only having to stoop a little to clear the ceiling. The place was full of the strong, earthy smell of wolf, and as his eyes adjusted to the darkness, he could make out a dim red glow ahead.

The glow, it turned out, came from a small pile of glowing coals in a rough brazier, a little circle of stones in the center of the large chamber he was now led into. The dull red light was barely enough for him to see by, but he could feel the size of the room by the echoes and the feel of the air. The cave was at least as big as one of his people's lodges, dug deep into the earth, and the darkness swallowed the ceiling above him, where there must have been a smoke-hole for the little fire-ring. This strange underground lodge must have been at least 25 paces around, and all along that wall sat silent wolves, their eyes reflecting glowing embers as they watched him.

One Arrow stood his ground in that strange place while his mind whirled. Part of him was terrified, the animal instinct of a soft and fangless creature staring sudden death in the face. But a greater part of him, a part that had been growing steadily stronger since his awakening, knew he was not here as a victim, a meal for hungry predators. This was his initiation, he knew. It was the formalization of a process that had begun when he was pulled half-alive from that evil hole in the ground and revived with a shared kill. This was his induction into the brotherhood of the wolves, and in the red gloom of the cave he could almost hear his heart beating in anticipation.

One of the wolf-shadows on the wall stepped out into the dim glow of the coals. It was the oldest wolf One Arrow had seen, a one-eyed old hunter with a grizzled coat and one back leg that dragged when he walked. The man could feel the power of this wolf-elder as he approached, a strength of spirit that had nothing to do with the feeble old bones that carried it; One Arrow knew instantly that he was a shaman of great power, a medicine man among wolves. The wolf looked for a moment at the man's injured leg, then turned his single eye upwards to the man's face.

That look was a spear piercing his soul; in an instant that one eye had seen everything that was in his heart and mind, and had measured and judged it all just as quickly. The old wolf sighed deep in his chest, a dry and rattling sound, and carefully sat down with a creak of aged joints. He looked the man in the eye once more, and uttered a sharp series of snarls and growls. The silence in the room thickened; they were waiting for something, and One Arrow thought it wisest to keep quiet, stand still and wait along with them.

The silence grew longer, and One Arrow began to sense a growing feeling of what seemed like awkwardness or embarrassment. The old wolf sighed again as he closed his good eye and stretched.

"So. You don't understand yet," the wolf shaman said, in a growling voice that seemed to claw at his old throat as he spoke. "Sit down, man. I will make you to understand more quickly."

Even after all his strange experiences, even with the new sense of belonging he'd found with his rescuers, One Arrow was shocked to hear a wolf speaking to him. He staggered backward a bit, bringing a fresh flash of pain from his leg.

"You...you can talk?" he asked, knowing he sounded stupid even as the words came out of his mouth.

"Yes, yes I talk," the wolf snarled irritably, glaring up at him with that piercing spear of an eye. "Everything talks. But can everything listen? No. Look, here is a man. I say, 'Sit down, man' and the man is still standing. I will try again. Sit *down*, man."

Stunned, One Arrow sank to the packed dirt floor of the wolves' underground lodge, the pain in his leg forgotten in his amazement. The shaman coughed and nodded.

"Good. Man-talk hurts my throat, even worse than crow-talk, so I must make you understand us wolves. You would learn by yourself, after a time, but men are slow learners. Now I will tell you something." The shaman's single eye was a burning flame as the old wolf leaned in close. "You are a dead man."

One Arrow could only stammer and stare, not knowing how to reply.

"Yes, dead! Dead to men. Dead to everything else too, if this one"—the elder gestured with his muzzle toward One Arrow's escort—"had not made you to live again. Now you are to be a brother to wolves. Understand?"

One Arrow nodded, dazed. "Yes. I understand."

"Huh. Maybe so. Maybe not. If not, you will soon." The one-eyed wolf barked a laugh. "Your heart is changing, yes. But your body is the same. Can't run, can't see, can't hear, can't smell. Dull claws, blunt teeth. But we will change the body to match the heart. Now."

He turned toward the ring of stones and kicked a small pile of leaves onto the glowing coals. Instantly they began to smolder, and the room began to fill with a pungent smoke that seemed to seep into One Arrow's skin even as it filled his lungs. Through the dense smoke, the shaman's eye glowed like a yellow beacon as, one by one, the wolves in the room began to howl their sacred song.

Rising and falling it went, a single song in a dozen parts. The dry plants on the little pile of coals burned out and the smoke cleared, but still the song remained in the red darkness, surrounding One Arrow as he sat hypnotized by its patterns. The old wolf-shaman leaped and danced, barking and whining his medicine chant in counterpoint to the droning howl of the singing wolves. One Arrow was lost in the wolf magic, fixed in place, feeling the power of this ancient tribe flowing into his weak body.

The chanting and singing grew steadily louder, until he thought it would burst his head, but he couldn't have moved his hands to cover his ears even if he'd wanted to. As it grew louder, though, it became somehow clearer; One Arrow could make out every wolfish voice in the howling chorus, could hear each detail of sound from a dozen animal throats.

The ears, the ears, he has the ears...

Joy filled him as he realized he could understand every word of their song, could comprehend every subtle shift of meaning in the wolf-words. Still he sat, as the song continued and the light of the glowing coals grew brighter. So bright, in fact, that they soon lit the whole room. The chamber had become bright as day, and the shadows fled to reveal his brothers in every detail of face and fur.

The eyes, the eyes, he has the eyes...

And the smell of that place, the mingling of the sweet tang of burning grasses and the individual scents of the gathered wolves, each one as unique as a face or a name. He knew these wolves, his people now, and knew he would never forget them, that he could follow them across the whole world if he had to. And he could smell blood in the air too, the old blood from the elk the big gray wolf had killed to feed him in his weakness. He was suddenly very hungry.

The nose, the nose, he has the nose...

Elation filled him as the medicine-song reached a fever pitch, a climax of joyful howling. The restraining force that had held him motionless snapped away and sent him into his new life, feeling light as a feather, solid as a rock. Running his long tongue across his parched lips, he felt his razor teeth and the points of his killing fangs. Flexing his hands, he felt needle-sharp claws pressing into leathery pads. Raising his shaggy head, he felt his howl joining the song of his brothers.

The voice, the voice, he has the voice...

The clouds that stretched to every horizon had kept their rain all day, holding it like a threat. It would come soon, though, the wolf-man knew. The hidden sun was going down and the damp was rising up. A perfect night for the work he had to do.

He took a deep breath of the dusk air that was heavy with the smell of coming storms, and even heavier with the smell of fresh buffalo blood. How many other perfect nights had there been since he'd joined his new people? Too many to bother counting; every night was a perfect night, it seemed. If it was dry, there was hunting where the game went to drink. If it was wet, it made for easy tracking. Everything happened as it happened, and wolves made the best of it all.

He'd hunted and he'd scavenged, and there was pride in both. He'd chased antelope for miles on his tireless legs, glorying in his body's power and the sharpness of his senses. He'd taken elk with tooth and claw, and used those same weapons to defend his status in the pack. That was good and right, the way of his people. It was wonderful, this new life he'd been given.

He raised up his right arm and studied it in the dying light. Coarse gray-brown fur covered its powerful ropes of muscle and tendon, and wicked claws topped the long fingers of the huge padded paw. He brought those fingers to his face and felt along the line of his bone-crushing jaws with their needle teeth, felt the fur of his muzzle extend down over his thick cords of neck muscle and down to his chest. There his claws stopped, as they always did, to touch the wolf's-tooth necklace he still wore, his last connection to the murdered man he once was.

He was brought out of his thoughts by a snort of laughter from beside him, and turned to glare at his companion. The big gray wolf was obviously bored of waiting in the long grass for night to fall, and when he got bored he liked to playfully tease his two-legged friend.

"Are you admiring your beautiful face again, Wolf-Man?" He-Howls-First asked in a growled whisper. "You're like a woman! How many times do I have to tell you before you'll believe me? You're a fine specimen of wolfkind, from the shoulders up at least.

"Or," he continued as he noticed the string of teeth and beads the half-man cradled in his leathery palm, "are you worried about that thing again? Forget it! Old Eagle-Took-His-Eye said you must keep it as long as you want it, and he spoke well. Nobody cares that it's made of teeth; I think it's a very funny joke. I'd probably have a necklace too, if I had the two-legs' medicine for making things. Maybe you can make me one someday, out of men's finger-bones, eh?"

He-Howls-First laughed again, and the wolf-man who was one called One Arrow couldn't help but laugh along. He thought about what their laughter would sound like to his former people whose camp was just beyond this big hill, and laughed even harder. How could they know that those wolves in the distance were giggling about making jewelry out of their bones?

"Maybe I'll do that," he said when they'd quieted themselves, and realized that he'd have no problem stringing a dead man's knucklebones on a string as a present to his friend; it would be powerful medicine. The thought brought back some of his introspective mood, and he leaned back into the grass of the hillside.

He-Howls-First yawned, taking a big gulp of air, and licked his chops. "Ah! Just smell all that fresh meat, brother. Doesn't it just make your mouth water?"

The wolf-man admitted that it did, even as his rumbling stomach answered for him. His former people had coralled and butchered a large number of buffalo, a very good take, and the scent drifted from miles away. The thrill of the hunt and the rush of a big kill was one thing, but an easy meal of delicious scraps and entrails couldn't be passed up on the hungry prairies.

How far I've come, the wolf-man thought. He had a man's skills and a man's knowledge still, but it was as if it was all kept in a pouch in his heart separate from who he really was. What connection did he have with the dead One Arrow? Hadn't that man already left his people long before a wolf pulled him out of a hole, back when he'd taken his wives to live apart? He had tried so hard to live right in his old world, had cared about the ways of his people to the point where he would rather leave than bear the embarrassment of disruption or impropriety. And now here he was, stalking in the grass with the wolves and drooling over the aroma of raw buffalo, waiting for darkness to fall so he could steal the leavings of his former people.

The strange thing was, it didn't really bother him; what bothered him was that he still had any misgivings at all. He was part of the wolf tribe now, and it wasn't right that there should be any part of his spirit still living in the lodges of the Blackfoot. But there was good food for his people to be had down there, and his people were counting on the man in him, the master of tools and traps, to get it for them.

He thought about the construction of the buffalo corral, the *pis'kun*. How many had he helped build? A big, circular wooden enclosure made of strong timbers, the *pis'kun* had a wooden ramp leading up over the wall. The people would drive the buffalo up the ramp, and the great hairy beasts would drop into the corral and run in circles as more of their kind joined them, until the whole enclosure was packed with confused animals. The people could then take their time killing them with arrows, and all the butchering was done right then and there, so much meat that it often took a long time to take away and prepare properly.

This is what caused problems for his brother wolves, and the coyotes and foxes too. The men knew that so much meat was irresistible to the hungry animals, and after they'd removed the buffalo ramp they graciously left convenient holes in the timber walls of the *pis'kun* by which scavengers might enter—every one of which was rigged with a deadly snare. It was an easy way for the people to get wolf hides and fox furs—and teeth like the ones the wolf-man still wore on a string around his shaggy neck.

Tonight, though, there would be no snares. Tonight he would go down and draw out the nooses, and spring the snares, and there would be a feast that would be sung about by wolves—and all their little brothers—for a very long time. As the last blush of light faded in the west and the first spatters of rain began to fall, the wolf-man knew it was time to get to work.

"With the dark and the rain, all the men will want to be in their lodges," the wolf-man said to his raiding partner, whose fur bristled with excitement. "Let's go down and get us some meat!"

The *pis'kun* was some distance from the Blackfoot camp, and there were no guards to be seen—or heard, or scented—as the two comrades crept up to the delicious-smelling enclosure. Even better, none of the snares had yet been sprung. He-Howls-First and the wolf-man had been certain they would find at least one stupid fox who couldn't help himself hanging by its neck. With his friend trotting silently beside him, the wolf-man went from snare to snare, making each trap safe.

As he was disarming one of the bigger snares—this one clearly meant to catch wolves—the wolf-man looked over to see He-Howls-First watching him intently, and what he saw disturbed him. The big gray-furred wolf was gazing in wonder at the working of the half-man's clawed

fingers as they handled the ropes. The look he wore was like that of a child amazed at some simple sleight-of-hand or shadow puppetry, and it made the transformed man angry that his rescuer, teacher and best friend should be so much in awe; it reminded him of how separate from his brothers he truly was.

Still, he made all the entryways safe and He-Howls-First sped back into the grass to call all the other animals that were waiting to feast. Soon there was a crowd of wolves, foxes and coyotes gathered in and around the *pis'kun*, trying very hard—but not very successfully—to be quiet as they gobbled as much meat as they could and then made off with as much as they could carry. If the one called Wolf-Man had been a curiosity before, now he was a legend. When at last the shouts of men caused the few remaining scavengers to bolt into the rainy night, there was hardly a bone left unpicked in the *pis'kun.*

The wolf-man sat behind a long, low hill, munching slowly on a delicious strip of good back-fat as the night rain intensified, his companion having gone farther up to the top of the rise to watch the confusion at the *pis'kun*. His keen ears picked up the happy sounds of his brothers who had scattered with their meaty loot—cheerful barks and noises of satisfaction. They were all amazed at how easy it had been to make off with so much food, all thanks to the Wolf-Man's human skills; for the first time, there was a consistent source of effortless feasting on the prairie. The constant search for food was the first concern of all things, and the wolf-man knew that any number of these hungry creatures would gladly give up the constant cycle of hunting and scavenging to follow his lead as he made corral after corral safe for raiding. The wolf-man couldn't blame his brothers—a full belly was a full belly— but still he was troubled. This didn't feel *right*.

He-Howls-First was chuckling with glee as he peered over the top of the hill and watched the confusion of the men below, listening to their confused and angry talk. "Wolf-Man," he sighed, rolling back to flop prone on the ground, "that was the most fun I've ever had, and the best meal I've ever eaten. And your skill with those snares! I never guessed, when I pulled you out of that hole, that it would be this good. We *must* do this again!"

"Yes," the wolf-man replied with a sigh and a hint of sadness that puzzled his friend. "Yes, I suppose we must."

The Blackfoot camp was in turmoil. Over the course of the season, the people had twice built the *pis'kun*, had twice captured and killed a great number of good buffalo, and twice had had their traps disarmed and the wolves and coyotes allowed in to steal meat. Once might have been explainable—maybe the snares had been poorly set, or someone had played a particularly cruel prank. But twice? It couldn't be an accident, and it was almost unthinkable that it could be a prank; the season was ending, supplies were dwindling and any twisted joker in the tribe would starve just as surely as everyone else should there be no meat to see them through the winter.

The worst part was not knowing who was troubling them. Was it some enemy from another tribe, breaking every tradition of honor and manhood by skulking in the night to starve another people? A witch or an evil spirit? A trickster coyote with a wicked mean streak? Nobody knew, and in the confusion of the ground around the sabotaged *pis'kun*, trampled by buffalo and men, the Blackfoot trackers stood no chance of picking out the tracks of the vandal. Fear was in the air.

Eventually the council of warriors and top men came up with a plan to trap this mysterious enemy, should he come again to allow the wolves to make off with the livelihood of the people. The next time the *pis'kun* was built and the buffalo driven, the hunters took far fewer than they might have—enough to live on, narrowly, a small enough number that all the meat could be butchered and taken from the corral in a single day of hard, quick work. In the enclosure the Blackfoot left only a single animal: a scabby, elderly bull, tough and ropy old meat. The men thought this was a great joke to the face of the unknown thief, a suitable reward for such sneaky actions.

That night, the conditions were perfect for their trap, with the wind blowing hard from the *pis'kun* toward their encampment. If the snare-wrecker came, he'd have to come from upwind, unable to catch the scent of the nearly empty corral. A band of warriors lay low in the long grass near the timber walls, flat on the ground in ambush. The chill night was clear, but only moderately bright under a half-moon, and the rush of the wind made it difficult to hear the small sounds that would give away a stealthy intruder. They'd have to rely on their eyes, or hope that the man—or thing—they were after made enough noise to be heard over the wind. Silent and watching, they waited for their enemy to make itself known.

They didn't have to wait long. Soon after the time when, on an ordinary night, the people back in the camp would have retired to their lodges and the comfort of their buffalo robes, the hidden Blackfoot guards heard strange animal growls carried clearly on the wind from the buffalo enclosure. They grew in volume and ferocity, becoming like snarls of rage, as if some animal was voicing its anger at finding that skinny carcass where it had expected an easy feast. Whatever was at the *pis'kun* was loud and unhappy, and the hidden Blackfoot shared uneasy looks. The warriors had just begun rising to a crouch to stalk forward and investigate when, abruptly, the snarling stopped. They froze in place, barely breathing, thinking that the creature had somehow heard their movement or caught their scent. Half-standing, they waited in silence until, from the direction of the nearby hills, they heard a sound none of them would ever forget.

It was a howl like no other, a nerve-wracking cry, half animal call and half warrior's yell, and it cut through the wail of the wind with a power that raised the hair on the motionless hunters' arms. In an unnatural, impossible mixture of the language of wolves and the speech of men, that weird voice howled out its frustration.

"*Aawwwww-hooooo! Bad-meat! Hoooo! Bad-you-give-us! Aaaawwwwhoooooo!*" A volley of answering howls from the dark hills joined in the chorus.

The Blackfoot warriors stared at each other in amazement. Here was a thing out of some of their oldest legends—a man-wolf. A creature that walked a path between the world of wolves and the world of men. It was a product of strange and terrifying medicine, and it was very near. Still, the bravery of the warriors was great, and the lives of their people were at stake. Summoning his courage, the leader of the little band stood up straight, spear held at the ready, and shouted back his own challenge through the barrage of howls.

"Wolf-man! Come forward! We would speak with you!"

A rumbling growl came from the silver-lit grass, in which nothing could be seen. When the growl rose to speak in the language of men, it was rough and horrible to hear, like each word had claws of its own that tore at the speaker's throat as they were spoken.

"Men! Why do you trick us like this? You trap my brothers at your corral, you kill so many good buffalo, you have many good things. Are you so mean and tight-fisted that you will deny us, and mock us with scabby old meat a crow wouldn't touch? Why are you so selfish, men?"

The leader of the men answered back plainly, as if explaining things to a small child; this strange being, he thought, might not know the ways of men. "Wolf-man, we cannot let you take what you wish, when you wish," he called. "Is it right that we do your hunting for you, and have nothing? You and you brothers are great hunters in your own right. Is it right that we let you rip and ruin the hides and furs of the buffalo? You and your brothers have furs of your own to keep you warm, and we do not. Wolf-man, when you take the buffalo, you take our lives."

There followed a long silence from the grass. When the wolf-man spoke again that painful voice was softer, more hesitant. "You...you speak well, " he growled, slowly. "I had...forgotten...how it is with men."

"Forgotten?" the man replied. "So then you were once a man? Come forward, and let us see you and speak with you."

"Very well," came the growling response. "Let us speak." There was a rustling in the grass, a shadow of movement, and the wolf-man was there before the stunned Blackfoot, loping across the buffalo-trampled ground with long, swift strides.

Their good, sharp spears seemed like children's toys when they saw the power of the being that faced them. Tall he was, and broad, with shoulders and arms like the branches of a great tree. His fearsome wolf's head was filled with white teeth like daggers, and his long arms— covered, like his head and shoulders, in a coat thick gray fur—sported clawed hands, or paws, so large they could crush a man's head in a single grip. From the shoulders down he was like a man, though strangely hairy and tanned dark by sun and weather. His legs looked like they could knock a tree down with one kick, and his chest was thick with muscle. And against that chest hung his only adornment: a simple necklace of wooden beads and wolves' teeth.

Seeing the man-made trinket, one of the party of men cried out in recognition. "One Arrow!" he shouted. "One Arrow, is it you?" The other warriors stared wide-eyed; they too had recognized the necklace of their former comrade.

"One Arrow?" the wolf-man rumbled. "Yes, that is what I was called by men, when I knew you. I have forgotten much, it seems."

"But...but you were lost," the man stammered, as shocked by his friend's return as by his wolflike appearance.

"I mean, your wives...they came back to our camp crying and tearing their hair, wailing that you had disappeared on the hunt."

"Lost?" The mighty half-man shook his muzzled head with a snort that might have been a laugh. "No, not lost. Dead. Dead and buried, deep in the ground. There was no escape, only darkness, until my brothers the wolves gave me a new life."

The wolf-man bared his teeth in a blood-chilling grin. "There are two women in your camp who are very skilled trappers. You should have had their help guarding your *pis'kun.* Maybe they could have caught me a second time."

The men realized what their former companion was saying, and began to forget their fear of this strange wolf-man in their anger over what had happened, at being lied to, at having sheltered evil in their lodges for so long. "This is an outrage!" the captain cried, his eyes flashing in indignation. "Will you go now to punish your wicked wives, One Arrow?"

"No!" The wolf-man's sharp bark of denial caused the men to jump back a pace. Seeing their fear, the shaggy hunter who had once been a man softened his tone. "No. I am not One Arrow, and I have no wives. I am called Wolf-Man by my brothers, and I have no say in the affairs of your people. But you do speak well; there must be an accounting. Give One Arrow's wives to the council of *I-kun-uh'-kah-tsi*, to your Societies of Warriors; you will know what should be done with them."

At this, the band of Blackfoot stared at each other in yet another kind of wonder. The man they had known as One Arrow had been merciful, to the point where he was ridiculed by some for being soft. It was this quality of mercy that had led him to leave the camp of his people to spare his wives the punishments their society would inevitably have demanded. The justice of the *I-kun-uh'-kah-tsi* would show no such mercy.

"Now," sighed the wolf-man, "I leave you in peace. I know now where I belong, and how things must be between wolves and among men. Farewell, men; I will not trouble your snares again."

With that, the strange creature of two worlds turned and began striding back to the hills, picking up speed as he loped through the grass on powerful legs. As the men watched him go, the wolf-man brought his body lower as he ran, bringing his great swinging arms closer to the ground with each step. As he ran up and over a hill some distance away, before he was lost to their sight forever, it seemed to the wondering Blackfoot that his shape was exactly that of a running wolf.

It was a long time before the men moved from where they stood, before they walked back to the camp to convene the warriors' societies and tell the story of One Arrow. When they finally turned to go, the man who had first recognized One Arrow stayed behind and followed the wolf-man's trail to investigate something that had caught his eye as the unfortunate creature had run back to his new brothers.

There, on the buffalo-trampled ground, he found it—a loop of deerhide, snapped at the knot, its scattered cargo of simple beads and hunters' teeth shining polished in the light of the moon and the stars.

A Fox in the Cathouse

Fast and agile, bright-eyed and alert, quick and cunning—
all around the world the fox is known as a trickster, a
prankster, a maker of mischief. But with creatures of legend,
especially those that walk among humans, playfulness has a
way of shading into maliciousness and jokes become
deadly—or worse. So it is that werefoxes, supernatural
beings that can take the form of both fox and man—or,
more frequently, of woman—are considered as dangerous as
werewolves and other shapeshifters of a more violent and
predatory sort.

In its behavior, a werefox is likely to have more in com-
mon with fairies and other mischief-making spirits than
with their more bloodthirsty cousins. Though they operate,
like most shapeshifters of legend, under strict magical rules
regarding what they can and can't do, they also extend their
own rules to the humans they come in contact with—they
tease, they test, they set challenges, rewarding those who pass
their tests and punishing those who fail. Of course, given the
lighthearted nature of these creatures, many of their stories
end with a human victory and an outsmarted fox running
for the hills. Those that beat a werefox at its games might
not rest too easy, though; these animal tricksters tend to have
long memories, and they bear grudges as much as they
remember kindnesses.

The price of getting on the bad side of a shape-changing
fox (for, more often than not, these creatures are foxes that
assume human shape rather than the other way around) is
usually less lethal than the price of an encounter with a

werewolf; slighted werefoxes are more likely to leave destitution, disaster or disfigurement of some sort. Often, the punishment for not meeting these cunning spirits' standards is simply the bitter knowledge of a missed opportunity.

Hence the many "animal wife" stories in which werefoxes figure. In these legends, a fox-woman is either willingly (as repayment for a kindness) or unwillingly (through such means as capture of the creature's magical fox-skin) entered into marriage with a human man. The husband, especially in cases where his supernatural bride is a willing partner, may not even be aware of his wife's true nature. As a condition of the marriage, the fox will set certain taboos—perhaps the husband is not to watch her while she dresses or undresses herself, or maybe the fox-bride must be given leave to go away on undisclosed errands on certain days of the year, or of each month. The marriage may be brief or it may last many years, but inevitably the foolish (or drunken) husband breaks the taboo and his magical wife—along with any children that may have been born into the household— is lost to him forever.

Like werewolves, werefoxes are often cursed creatures, beings to be pitied. This is especially true of foxes in Asian folklore, where they are the most common shapeshifting creatures of legend. The werefox curse, however, is inclined to have a more spiritual dimension. In many cases the fox is a creature trapped between worlds, a lost spirit bound to walk the earth in this form until certain conditions are met that will redeem it, free it from its bondage and allow it to travel on to—whatever comes next.

The following is one such story. Based on an old legend from Japan, a land whose body of werefox, or kitsune, *folklore*

*is broad and deep enough to fill a library on its own, it's a tale
of a man whose path to righteousness leads him into sweet
temptation, and a fox-woman whose search for a righteous
man leads her through the lowest circles of society.*

The air hung close over the rugged peaks, heavy with heat
and moisture—"mosquito hot" was the term people
used. The constant rhythmic trill of summer cicadas
came from everywhere, and there was no breeze to give
old Isamu any relief as he struggled, hauling himself with
his staff, up the steep hill-path for the second time that
day. With what breath he could spare, he asked Buddha
for strength.

It was a combination of mercy and honesty that drove
the old woodcutter back up this way when he might otherwise have been resting after a long day in the woods,
relaxing in the bathhouse and letting the scalding water
soothe the ache from his joints. Mercy, toward the she-fox
he'd found caught in a trapper's snare; honesty, toward
the man who'd caught her. He'd heard her a long way off,
crying, and when he came across her she'd seemed to have
begged him for release. But as much as mercy was a
virtue, robbery was a sin, so Isamu had taken his creaking
body back down the mountain to his poor little cottage,
pulled his hidden purse from its place deep in the rough
thatch of his roof, and plucked out one of his few carefully
saved silver coins. He could feel its weight in the pocket of
his robe; the vixen would have her life and freedom, and
the trapper would have a fair price for his lost fox-pelt.

She was no longer crying when he came to the place where she was trapped, but sat watching him silently, stock-still but for an occasional quivering spasm of her trapped paw. Isamu knelt and opened the snare, and the freed animal bounded away to perch on a nearby fallen log. She licked at her injured limb, raising her head often to watch the woodcutter with liquid eyes. Isamu thought it odd that the fox hadn't run off, but shrugged and bent back to the trap, tying his small coin there with a scrap of cloth. He stood with an aching grunt, and turned to head for home.

As he stood, the vixen pricked up her ears and jumped off the log, favoring the paw that had been trapped. Capering ahead of the old man, then back again, she stayed with him, follow-leading, much of the way down the path. Isamu was charmed by the vixen's company, but wary—*kitsune*, after all, were unpredictable creatures, and the omen of having a fox keep company with you could be read either way. Where the forest trail opened up into cultivated land, the quick little animal scampered off to the right, looking straight at the weary old man and giving three sharp barks before disappearing back into the undergrowth. Puzzled and hoping Buddha would help him come to understand this strange encounter, Isamu headed for a hot bath and home.

Three days later, resting in the doorway of his little hovel after another long day of cutting wood and hauling the bundles down from the hills, Isamu spotted a young woman approaching in a simple but exquisitely made orange-brown silk robe. As she drew near, the old man could see that she was a girl of exceptional beauty. Her skin was fine and glowing, her lips like blossoms, her walk as gentle and sensuous as a sapling in the breeze. At first, the woodcutter thought she might be a lady-in-waiting in some noble's entourage, who had somehow gotten herself lost while passing the nearby village. But as she came nearer Isamu got a good look at her eyes—perfect almond eyes, beautifully liquid—and he knew exactly what it was that was approaching his house.

His old body electric with fear, his inner voice rattling off prayers as fast as he could come up with them, Isamu nonetheless remembered his manners. Bowing low, he addressed the girl he knew to be *kitsune*.

"Good afternoon, honored lady. Your arrival is a blessing; please be welcome in my most unworthy home. But, pray tell me what one such as I might offer, that you honor me with this visit?"

The girl in the colors of autumn returned his bow with a tiny, perfect smile. "Forgive the rudeness I am committing, master woodsman, but I believe you know me, and have some idea why I have come to your honorable door on this day."

Isamu's head rang with a thousand bells of warning. "Forgive my ignorance, but if the honored lady would please explain?"

Her smile widened, showing a row of teeth like pearls as the girl gave the smallest of glad laughs. Isamu's heart almost broke to hear its music. "Do you not know me, kind one? It is I whom your mercy saved from doom three short nights ago, whose life you bought with honest silver. I know you have no wife, so I come to you now to repay you as I may, to offer myself into your service."

With this she bowed low once more, a spring willow bending to the ground.

The fireside stories of his grandfather and his grandfather's grandfather flashed through the mind of the stunned woodcutter. The gifts and blessings of the *kitsune* are not to be taken lightly; if at all possible, as sound wisdom has it, they should not be taken at all. Throwing himself at the marvelous creature's feat, Isamu cried out in protest. "Great fox spirit! Blessed creature of magic! I am unworthy of this great gift, having only performed that service to which the Lord Buddha calls us. I am honored many times over by your visit, but I am but a poor woodcutter and unfit to be served by one such as yourself. Give me only your blessing, and consider your debt paid a thousand times over."

The girl's face took on a look of solemn consideration, but amusement sparkled in those eyes of flowing copper. "I beg you, kind one, please do not abase yourself before one such as I. But it is true what you say: you *are* poor, as the world reckons riches. Allow me, at least, to put you on the path to wealth."

The old man looked up from the dirt, not understanding the mischievous glint of irony in the beautiful fox-maiden's upturned mouth. Warily, he replied, "How might you set me on that path, honored spirit?"

"Come to me tomorrow morning, in your best sandals and finest robe, at the point where three days ago I left you. Follow where I lead, honored cutter of wood, and you have the word of the *kitsune* that good fortune will be yours."

The solemn promise of a fox-spirit is not a light thing, and Isamu, humbled, bowed low to the ground once more. When he lifted his head from the packed and swept dirt of his houseyard, there was no one to be seen. Bewildered, he entered his little shack to begin mending his best robe.

The next morning, self-conscious in his worn but well-made robe and sturdy sandals, Isamu made his way past fields and rice-paddies to the appointed spot, half wondering if he was chasing after a dream—or, if it wasn't a dream, if he was chasing after his own doom. But he heard the bark of a fox, and there where the path entered the woods sat the vixen, peering at him through the grass. She barked again, three times, and disappeared up the path. Without looking back—somehow, he felt he must not—he followed the sleek little animal into the spider-webbed shade of the hillside thickets.

The fox led him onward through the forest, up one mountain and down the other side, through paths he didn't know, or had perhaps forgotten from his youth. When another traveler was seen ahead the vixen would disappear into the brush, only to pop up again farther down the road, beckoning him with a sharp little bark. It didn't take long to travel farther than the old woodcutter had ever been from the valley that was his home, and still they walked. When he was hungry, Isamu—who, as the Buddha taught, had long ago sworn off meat—ate berries and other fruits of the forest. When he was thirsty, he drank from cool running streams. At night, he slept under a sky undampened by rain. And, always, the little fox led him onward. For days, the odd pair traveled in this manner.

At noon on the fourth day, they crested a tall hill and came upon a green-sided valley in which rested the largest city—the first city—Isamu had ever seen. Beyond the tangled network of streets and alleys, punctuated with the spires of red pagodas, was the broad curve of the bay, glittering in the sun and dotted with boats. Beyond that stretched the wide ocean, green islands in the distance. Isamu could have stood and absorbed the view until the sun had gone, but the vixen's bark brought him back to his task, and he followed the bushy tail as it once again flashed down into the close shade of the forest path.

At last, two miles from the edge of town by Isamu's guess, they arrived at a pleasant grove that contained an ancient shrine to Inari, goddess of foxes. Isamu sat down with a tired sigh as the little vixen barked three times again and darted through the gate to the shrine—again, he somehow felt he was not to follow. He was near to dozing off when he heard the crunch of sandals on the gravel path and looked up to see the young woman who had visited him at his cottage emerging from the gate. The woodcutter leaped to his feet with a popping of joints: if the fox-maiden had been lovely before, now she was radiant. Dressed in an embroidered robe of finest silk, hair adorned simply and in the finest taste, her beauty left nothing for the old man to do but stand and stare.

She smiled and laughed a little at his dumbstruck expression, but spoke as if four days hadn't passed since their last conversation had ended. "Behold," she said, with that glint of mischief again in her eye, "I am your daughter, Nanashi, and you are my father, who once was wealthy but is now forced to barter his daughter so that the rest of his household may live. Take me now to the richest brothel in the city, and sell me for a hefty purse of gold."

At this, the woodcutter threw himself to his knees on the gravel path. "No! Sell you into their filthy clutches? I would sooner have nothing, and live as I have these past four days or starve and die!"

Again the fox-maiden laughed, and it was the sound of silver coins in a bronze alms cup. "Fear not, kind one; no flesh-peddler will keep me long. As soon as I might, I will once again assume my...other shape, and be gone from that place. You will have the wealth your virtue deserves, evil men shall have some small punishment for their wicked intentions and there will be no stain on your noble soul." She briefly showed those pearly teeth in a wicked little smile. "It is, you must agree, an excellent jest."

Isamu felt the chill of ghost-touch run down his arms again as he was reminded of what it was that he was dealing with. He was involved now, whatever might become of it. With a silent appeal to the Buddha, he let out a great sigh of resignation and offered his arm to the beautiful young maiden who stood smiling on the path to the fox-goddess's shrine.

And so it was that "Yoshiharu Okano," a formerly wealthy grain-trader ruined by vice and poorly chosen associates, came to stand in the entryway to the city's most opulent house of public women, a place where the music and feasting never stopped, where fat merchants and dissolute nobles poured money as fast as they poured wine, in order to negotiate the sale of his youngest daughter.

When the brothel-owner saw the fox-woman, his bulging eyes popped even further out of his round face, and that face took on a new and deeper shade of red. With great sweeps of his meaty hands, he ushered the woodcutter and the fox-maiden into his lush receiving-room. As Isamu spun a story of cursed luck and lost wealth that he remembered from a cautionary tale his grandmother had told him, the chubby owner mopped at his sweating brow with a square of fine silk worth more than the woodcutter could hope to make in two years breaking his back in the hills. Isamu could have been reciting nursery rhymes or the cargo list of some freight barge for all the fat man cared—he and his retinue of sycophants and hangers-on only had eyes and ears for the beautiful girl in embroidered golden silk.

"Yes, yes, of course," he muttered, some moments after Isamu had finished speaking. He hadn't taken his frog-eyes off the girl who'd been introduced to him as Nanashi—an obviously false name, he knew—and his greedy mind was busy calculating the river of money this beautiful creature could make flow from the pockets of his upper-end clientele. "A terrible thing to have happen, just terrible. Well, we'll take good care of her here. This is a high-class establishment, Okano-san, yes, high class..." His voice trailed off and he ran his eyes once more over the vision of loveliness that knelt demurely, head bowed, on the thick reed-mat floor. Smiling lecherously, he clapped his hands.

And aide steeped up quickly with a writing kit, and the owner seized a brush with a flourish, hurriedly drawing up one of his standard bills of sale. "Now this is the usual arrangement, Okano-san, strictly routine, you see? Three years' service from your lovely daughter, in exchange for which I will pay out immediately the sum of 30 measures of gold. My man Kasuga, over there, will have your money when you depart my establishment."

Isamu wanted nothing more than to be out of the sickly, perfumed atmosphere of that wicked place, to be back the way he came and safe cutting wood until his span of days ran out, to be free of foxes and their tricky plans. He reached out for the brush the man held out to him.

"Stop, father!" It was the fox-maiden, crying out. Isamu looked back to where she knelt, head bent low to the floor. Though he couldn't see her face, the old man felt sure there was a wicked smile in her eyes. "You know I will obey you in this, as I have always obeyed you, but pray think of the sum you are accepting. Already our house is brought low; I beg you not to lower us further by valuing your daughter at such a pittance."

Isamu blushed furiously, speechless. This was a fox spirit, and not in truth his daughter, but it was still shocking to hear a woman speak so when business was being conducted by men. The fat man's little court, too, was silent. The only one still making a sound was the maiden in autumn-gold silk.

"Honored sir, please forgive my rudeness here in your own house, but I believe I misheard something you said. Tell me, did you not say 60 measures of gold just now?"

There were a few scattered gasps from the gold-diggers and yes-men gathered in the brothel-keeper's reception chamber. Such cheek, from one who was being sold into bondage to a whorehouse! The owner, however, was an experienced man of business—it was his profession, and his joy in life. He knew when he was facing a real wheeler-dealer, woman or not, and his reflexes carried him into the ancient dance of the give-and-take.

"Sixty! My descendants not yet born would curse me for a fool and spit on my name if I paid a penny more than 40, for I would be robbing them just as surely as if I were to pick their pockets myself!"

The fox-maiden was still speaking demurely, her eyes on the floor. Isamu had never set eyes on a more gifted performer. "Father, forgiveness, please, for being so forward. I know matters of money are not a woman's place, but I also know that the jasmine perfume I once wore when...when mother was still...when things were better...it cost easily ten a month. Am I not worth six small measures of perfume in the eyes of my father?"

The procurer's face was the red-purple of a pickled plum. He'd been in business long enough to know when he was the fish on the hook. Curse all women who are aware of their beauty! He had to have this girl! The big man slapped his hand on the table, setting the ink-jar rattling.

"I beg you! Have mercy on a poor man trying to make a living for his family! Fifty, and not a penny more!"

"Father," said the beautiful fox-girl, in a voice like a kitten's tail, "did we not see a fine-looking establishment some ways back on the road to this place? It seemed well kept and prosperous. Perhaps the master of that house has..."

"Gaaah! Enough!" The owner took up the brush again and savagely attacked the rice-paper contract, scrawling down the asked-for sum in brutal swipes. A calligraphy-master would blanch in shock to see the anger contained in those angry brushstrokes. "Sixty it is! Take your money and go, Okano-san! I just hope your daughter is as skilled in the womanly arts as she is in the business of men, or I'm ruined!"

As Isamu was hustled off the premises, unhappily clutching a pouch full of more money than he'd ever seen in his life, his so-called daughter was whisked upstairs by the brothel keeper's attendants. From screened chambers all around her came the sounds of flutes and stringed instruments, the sighs and squeals of the house's women, and the laughter and boasting of drunken men. Rich perfumes and incenses couldn't quite cover the odor of sweat and spilled drink. As she was led through the polished corridors, those she passed would stop and stare at this great beauty, the women filled with green envy, the men with red lust. If the fox-maiden's guide wondered at the hint of an amused smile on the new girl's lips—on this, the day of her sale, to be smiling!—she said nothing as she ushered her into the rooms of the mistress of dressing.

The brothel's wardrobe mistress, a plump woman on the downhill side of middle age, with the soul of an artist, could hardly contain herself when she saw the girl that knelt demurely in her antechamber. Here, she thought, was a girl worthy of her skills, a piece of perfect ivory her art would transform into a masterpiece. She wasted no time sweeping into action, calling out to servants for the best of the house's gowns and jewelry. In a whirlwind of silk the maiden was draped in kimono after precious kimono, each one a wonder of embroidery and worth a fortune. With careful eye, the mistress assembled not just a public woman's outfit, but a poem, a song, a harmony of woman and robe. At last, with the selection of the most exquisite of jewels and ornaments, her creation was ready for display.

Word travels quickly in the streets of any city's pleasure district, and the alleys of the town had been filled with gossip of the arrival of a new girl of exceeding beauty. The lane outside the brothel was already thronged with gawking rabble and the curtained litters of the rich and powerful when the fox-maiden made her appearance on the brothel's balcony. Usually when a new girl was exhibited there were catcalls, lewd comments and wolf-whistles from the crowd below. When Nanashi stepped out onto the high platform, the only sound was the sharp hiss of a collective gasp, followed by the babbling rustle of a whispering crowd.

The creature on the balcony was a vision of female beauty. In the late-afternoon sun, her almond eyes seemed to glow with their own molten light, while the light blush on her pale cheeks gave a counterpoint of girlish innocence. Her robe and ornaments had been chosen with the eye of a true master, perfect for the late summer season. The bright flower in her hair recalled the joys of spring, while her deep gold kimono, embroidered with leaves of olive and copper, spoke as a reminder of the autumn that would soon be upon them. The effect was to make a man feel his own mortality, even while his blood ran hot with desire for youthful beauty. Some who saw her felt tears come to their eyes, and there was a universal murmur of appreciation when one elderly man, in a voice choked with sentiment, was moved to improvise a traditional *haiku* poem:

Late-blooming flower
How cruel to speak of springtime
With winter so near

The bidding for the privilege of her company began immediately. Messengers ran back and forth between the servant-borne sedans of the wealthy and the brothel-keeper's agents in the courtyard, bearing pledges of ever-greater sums of money as the gathered crowd, who could only dream of sampling the pleasures of that palace of sin, watched in amusement. Some even began placing their own side-bets on the issue of which lusty spendthrift would win this greatest of prize beauties. The maiden had long gone from the balcony—it had taken only a moment's glimpse to start the unheard-of bidding frenzy—but still the men on the street cast their eyes up to that spot with looks of longing.

As the offers reached ruinous heights, the brothel-keeper wringing his hands and nearly weeping with joy and money-love, a representative of the provincial warlord's eldest son, flanked by two imposing men-at-arms, arrived bearing a heavy wooden coffer. Stepping up to the brothel's head agent, the prince's representative bowed briefly and opened the box he carried to display its contents. The agent's face went white and his eyes fairly flew out of his head as he looked at the sum being offered. After dropping almost to the ground and offering the most lavish thanks and praise, the owner's man hurriedly took the money-box into his arms and, still bowing, backed into the brothel. There was no question of further bidding: the mysterious, enchanting girl would belong to the prince this night.

The feast set for the prince and his ten companions was as lavish as the establishment could provide. The finest banqueting-room in the house, on a top floor cleared of all other guests, was appointed with the richest cushions and table settings and decorated in the most elegant style. Soft lamps were lit, and the most deliciously subtle of incenses were wafted into the room. The table was laid with rare delicacies and rice wine of exceeding quality. And the girls! The girls were, like the food and the furniture, the very best the brothel-keeper could make available. All were courtiers of the highest caliber, master musicians and conversationalists, trained in the arts of seduction and flattery—and all were, by anyone's standards, incredibly beautiful.

But, on that night, none could compare to the almond-eyed girl called Nanashi. The eyes of the prince and his friends were drawn to her as flowers to the sun— or moths to a flame. As her attentions turned this way and that, to one and then another, filling their *sake* cups and laughing brightly at their jokes and witticisms, the young men would alternately bask in the glory of her gaze, or shoot dark daggers at whichever of their friends was for the moment so blessed. Blood began to run hot, and the wine-cups never ran empty.

The other girls, meanwhile, envious of the new girl's power over the handsome young prince and his party, became more and more shameless in their attempts to draw the attention of the men their way. But their brazen innuendoes and seductive gestures served only to inflame the drunken passions of the young blades, whose jealous boasting and posturing became increasingly aggressive.

The feast was soon a fight waiting to happen, a gathering storm with the smiling, laughing Nanashi at its center.

It was then, with the atmosphere hot and thick with wine-soaked lust, that a sudden gust or draft from somewhere blew through the room, extinguishing all the lamps. The party was plunged into darkness and confusion. From the midst of the clatter of dishes and the squeals of women, the clear voice of the maiden cried out loudly:

"My prince! One of your guests has...has made free with his hands! Oh, make a light so that you may know this false friend, this snake you've taken to your breast— he is the one whose hat-tassel I have torn off!"

But before a lamp could be lit, the prince—who was just sober enough to know there would surely be blood among his men over this—shouted in the darkness, "Wait! We've all had too much to drink, and this was an indiscretion of the moment. Sometimes, it is better not to know a thing; let us all tear off our tassels and toss them on the table, and save a quarrel."

With that, the prince clapped his hands, and a candle was lit. There on the table, among the half-eaten delicacies and spilled wine, were ten silk cords, and around the table not a single hat still bore its ornament. The maiden, flushed and shaking with rage, sat clutching a tassel in one tiny white-knuckled fist and holding the front of her rumpled kimono closed with the other. One of the prince's men laughed out loud at this and began to sing, in a mocking tone, an old love-song about a lost hat. The other guests, relieved that the moment of tension had passed thanks to the prince's trick, made merry and joined in. Soon, the whole room, men and ladies, was singing and laughing—all except the insulted maiden.

"Bad enough my family's situation forced me to this life!" she cried, standing and knocking a wine vessel across the table. "But if insults like this are to go unavenged, even by the supposedly noble son of a noble man, then I choose not to live at all!" With that she slammed a screen aside and ran out onto the polished cypress balcony at the back of the house. Before any of the stunned party could follow, she'd cast the fine garments of the brothel into the swift-flowing river below and, taking once again her fox-shape, darted into a hidden riverside burrow.

Above, she heard the dismayed outcry of the prince as he came out onto the balcony to see a flash of rich golden cloth being carried fast away by the moonlit current of the river. An alarm was raised and, as the brothel keeper cried and tore his hair, boats were set out on the river to search for the lost maiden. All night the lovestruck prince and his remorseful companions combed the banks of that swift stream, but when the sun rose again all they had recovered was a single silken dressing robe. This the prince kept, a token of the radiant beauty that had shone once and then was snuffed out, a sad memento for the rest of his days.

Some time later, while the city was still buzzing with stories of the mysterious girl who had so briefly dazzled all who saw her, old Isamu was walking the village path toward where his new house was to be built. On the long journey back to his home he had considered what to do with the heavy weight of gold the crafty fox-maiden had pried out of the brothel-keeper's fat hands. He'd asked Buddha for guidance, but Buddha had nothing to say on the matter. He'd considered giving it all away in alms, but something told him he would be inviting more trouble if he didn't use the money as the fox-spirit had intended— to increase his material situation. So he'd bought good land near his old home, and commissioned himself a fine mansion. It was there he was walking, to oversee its construction, when he heard the gentle steps of a woman come up behind him.

He turned, and goosebumps sprang up along his arms: there, again, was the fox-maiden, in a shimmering kimono of bamboo-green. She smiled and stepped up beside him, keeping pace as he walked. What more did this dangerous thing of magic want from him?

"Have I not kept my word, master woodcutter?" she asked, gently.

"Yes, indeed you have," Isamu responded, warily. "I now have a large piece of good land in the district of my father and my father's father, and even now men are building me a fine house."

"So," she said brightly, "you are no longer a mere cutter of wood, but a man of substance and stature. And yet, what is a house without a wife, without a family?"

She stopped him with a touch on his elbow, turning him toward her. Isamu's mouth was dry, and his knees weak. He prayed for strength as he regarded the fox-maiden. The cicadas trilled in the fields and the trees rustled pleasantly in the refreshing breeze. Somewhere a farm wife was singing bits of an old song as she hung her washing. It was a beautiful day.

"Look at me, kind one," she said, her eyes pleading. Would you not take me now as your wife? Would you not bring me into that fine home being built for you?"

Isamu looked. She was perfection indeed. Graceful and sure, she moved like a swaying reed. Her eyes were clear and bright, golden in the sun. Her lips were...Isamu shook his head; she was the most beautiful woman a man could ever hope to see, and she was yet again offering herself to him. But she was as far beyond him as a cloud is beyond a stone. She was a creature of magic, of the spirit world, ancient and wise and wild, and he was a woodcutter, old and broken, a simple man with no learning other than the wisdom of years and the teachings of the Buddha. It could never be. Anguished, he threw himself down once more at the fox-woman's feet.

"No, wise one! Again you bless me with your offer, but this cannot come to pass. Does the rasping crow mate with the swan? Thanks to your craft, I have a house and some land, yes. But how many thousands of other men have exactly this? Forgive me if I am presuming too much, O beautiful one, but surely if you are to have any place in the world of humans it must be in the palaces and estates of a great man, and not in the home of a country farmholder. I am unworthy!"

"Please, do not kneel before me, sir." She bent and touched his cheek with cool fingers of ivory, gently leading him to his feet. Was that a look of joy in her eyes? "Will you do one thing more for me?"

Isamu nodded mutely, his expression glum. Why would this *kitsune* not release him from her schemes?

"Go back tomorrow to the city, to the brothel where you left me," she said. "Offer to buy back my contract, which the agreement provided for. Since the fat man cannot produce me, he will be obliged to make a damage payment to you for the loss of your daughter—do not take less than 200."

Before Isamu could argue or protest, the maiden gave a graceful little leap into the air. When she touched ground again, it was on the four feet of a fox. The vixen gave her usual salute of three sharp barks and sprang away into the green. For a long time, the former woodcutter stared at the spot where the last white flicker of the *kitsune*'s tail-tip had disappeared. At last he sighed and, shaking his head, continued on his way to where his house was being constructed. Why was Buddha testing him so?

A similar thought was on the brothel-keeper's mind two days later, as he sat in his gaudily decorated office and sweated over his accounts. Between the price he'd paid for the girl's term of service and the expense of the prince's lavish feast, that business with the maiden called Nanashi had nearly ruined him. He still had the prince's gold—the nobleman's son's heavy conscience would not let him take back the price he'd paid to have the girl—but it barely covered the food and drink the party had consumed. The greedy procurer had gone all-out with that banquet in the hopes of making a regular client of the lusty young prince, and instead his entire business was depressed, his house tainted by that night's events. He would have to pay a priest to perform a public exorcism.

Sixty measures of gold for a girl who would now entertain only water-spirits and river-ghosts—what a fool he'd been! He might as well have thrown the money into the stream himself, and saved himself a world of trouble. The fat man wrung his sweating hands in agony as he looked over his balance sheets. He prayed for further calamity to befall the household of Yoshiharu Okano, preferably of the terminal kind—if the old coot ever came for his daughter, that would be the end of everything.

At the sound of carriage wheels pulling up to his establishment, the brothel-keeper's head swung up from where it had been buried in his hands. It was just after noon-time, in the thick heat of the day. Who visits a house of pleasure when the sun is up? It wasn't unheard-of, of course; there were plenty of elderly fellows who had to take their companionship early, while they were still awake enough to enjoy the company. But somehow the owner was sure that wasn't the case this afternoon—he had a bad feeling. Wringing his hands as if trying to wash off his bad luck, he hurried out to his courtyard wondering what fresh hell the laughing gods had in store for him.

It gave Isamu a feeling of great pleasure to watch the blubbery brothel-keeper change color from his usual red to ash-white to deep purple when he stepped out into his courtyard to see old Okano waiting for him, but that feeling was replaced by shame at having taken joy from another's misery. Still, even the Enlightened One himself would have been amused at the sight of the wealthy pro-curer, usually a greasy fountain of silken words and sweet flattery, stammering and coughing, blinking in the sunlight, working his hands as if wrestling an invisible snake. *Buddha, forgive me,* thought the former woodcutter, *but this is going to be fun.*

"Greetings, honored master of this house," Isamu cried out in grand tones, bowing as elegantly as he could with his aged joints. "I pray thee, forgive the rudeness of my unexpected intrusion."

"Oh. Oh...O...O-Okano-san! I...I mean to say, we...this house, uh...w-welcome! Welcome, yes..." The man's voice trailed off in a strangled little sob. He looked as though his heart would burst from exertion.

"Master hosteler? Are you quite well? If I may say, you appear quite out of sorts. Perhaps this sun doesn't agree with one such as yourself, accustomed as you must be to the nighttime hours."

Isamu watched the sweating man's eyes dart from the fine carriage he'd arrived in, to the well-made silk robe around his frail shoulders, to the expensive new sandals on his feet. "Well...yes. Yes, yes...qu-quite well, Okano-san. I must say, you...you look in much b-better straits than when...when I last saw you."

"Oh, yes, and thank you for saying so," Isamu bowed. "After I returned home from the sad errand that last brought me to your door and discharged my unfortunate obligations with your generous payment, I received news that a cousin of mine had passed on and that, through an odd series of marriages and legacies, I had quite a tidy fortune coming to me. Are they not funny, my dear feastmaster, the tricks the gods play upon us?"

The brothel keeper was not amused; in fact, the beginnings of tears were forming in the corners of his eyes. He was shaking so hard Isamu half-expected to hear his greedy brains rattling in his head. Choked by terror, he could not reply, so the old woodcutter continued on.

"A thousand apologies if I am causing disruption to your fine house, but I am here to buy out my beloved daughter's term of service, as provided for in our contract." He pulled the rolled parchment document from his sleeve with a theatrical flourish. "My man at the carriage has your 60 measures of gold, along with interest plus something extra for your troub...why, my good man! Whatever is the matter?"

The fat man was a teakettle that had boiled over, shaking and bubbling, sweat pouring down his beet-red face to mix with the tears that now streamed freely from him eyes. "Oh...oh...oh..." he gibbered, eyes bloodshot and bulging.

"Sir, I'm sorry to be rude," said Isamu with relish, "but if you are going to have an attack or fit of some sort, I'd rather you did it after you've called my daughter out so we may be on our way."

At last, the boiling kettle exploded. The brothel-keeper flung himself to the ground at the old man's feet, groveling and scraping, staining the stones of the courtyard with sweat and tears. "Okano-san! Please, oh please, I beg your forgiveness. Your daughter, she...she is dead! Gone! Swept away by the river! Oh, I am sorry, Okano-san..."

The poor man trailed off into an stream of barely coherent apologies interspersed with bouts of begging. Isamu staggered back, clutching at his chest as if he'd been run through with a spear.

"Dead? Dead?" he said quietly, trying to put just the right catch in his voice. "Not ten days ago she was...she was...how? How did it happen?"

The pimp was weeping openly now, bawling like a frightened child. "Suicide, honored master! She...she said she could not go on living, and…and threw herself into the river! We looked for her, we looked, and the prince, but…"

Isamu flared up in towering anger. "Killed herself! My daughter was joy itself, my ray of hope in our troubles! And obedient in whatever she was called upon to do! If she killed herself, it was only because she was driven to it by unbearable ill-treatment! I call it murder! Murder!"

"Oh, please! I'm begging you, please, merciful master! Don't shout so!" A small crowd was beginning to gather at the entryway to the brothel's yard. "Keep the 60, and take another 60 besides! I am a dog! I am sorry!"

"'Keep the 60,' he says!" The old woodcutter was truly raging now, all the unreleased fury of a lifetime of peace bursting out to fill the walled court. " 'And another 60 besides'! Scum! Filth! Master of fraud and father of sin! You dare to buy my daughter's life as you bought her servitude, with the change from your filthy pockets? I denounce you! Murderer!"

"Please, gentle lord, have mercy!" The miserable flesh-peddler's tears had run dry. He was sobbing now, in ragged gasps. "Take…take a hundred! I cannot bring your daughter back, but take a hundred measures of gold in payment!"

Isamu didn't have to reach very deep into his soul to find contempt for the cowering thing that knelt at his feet. He turned his furious boil into a tight seethe, hissing his words though clenched teeth. "The man so ready with one hundredweight can just as easily find two."

The brothel-keeper looked up at the old man, blinking, eyes rimmed in livid red. "T-two hundred? Okano-san, you will destroy me!'

"It is my *intention* to destroy you, lord of all vice and perversion, just as you have destroyed my family, and all our joys and hopes for the future. My life is ashes, ashes and dust! I don't want your money for my gain, whore-master, but for *your* ruin!" Isamu was almost panting with exhaustion; his performance was more tiring than hauling firewood.

The pimp sagged, motionless as a weathervane in a sudden calm. "Very well, Okano-san," he said, sniffling a little. "How can I deny you?" He clapped his hands twice, two wet slaps, and an aide came running with a big money-box. The kneeling man opened it, took out and pocketed a few big coins, and lifted the heavy chest up to the woodcutter. "Take it and go, with whatever blessing such as I may give. And if you have any mercy in your heart, I beg you to pray it satisfies the spirits that have seen fit to plague me."

Isamu's manner softened, surprising the now-destitute pimp, and his voice took on a faraway tone. "I pray that it does, brothel-keeper. Oh, how I pray that it does."

It had been three days since he returned home a wealthy man, and Isamu sat in the doorway of his old hovel, looking up at the full moon and contemplating all that had happened to him. He liked it here, in this familiar place, close to the woods he'd worked and the hills he knew like the back of his gnarled hand. Buying it, and the land surrounding it, had been the first use he'd put the pimp's money to. He had more now than he'd ever wanted, more than he'd ever dreamed, more than he'd ever wanted to dream. He should have been happy, content; the fullness of this moon should have been the fullness of his joy.

But the strange business didn't feel finished. Every day felt like the second-last line of a poem, or a song with the final note left to be played—he couldn't believe he'd seen the last of the *kitsune* that had, in her gratitude, given him nearly everything a man could want. When he heard footsteps behind him, he'd jump and whirl, expecting to see that familiar beautiful face with its wicked little smile and sparkling eyes. When he heard a rustle in the undergrowth, he expected a sleek, long-tailed vixen to come darting out onto the path, barking in greeting. His every moment was filled with waiting, for her.

He heard a soft footstep behind him and to the right, on the path from the mountainside. He felt the familiar shiver up his arms, the chorus of bells in his ears. *Our thoughts are our prayers*, he reminded himself, smiling a little.

"Hello, wise one," he said, still gazing at the pregnant moon.

"Hello, kind one." Her voice was the soft burning of clean wood. "Have I not kept my word?"

"You have, O honored spirit. A thousand times, you have. Good fortune has, indeed, been mine."

"So, now you are no longer a mere farmholder. You are a wealthy man, with money to invest and the power it brings. Yet what is money and power without a wife, without a family to bear proudly your honored name?" The night insects chirped in the moonlit darkness. The hissing *sa-wa-wa* of the breeze-blown bamboo thickets whispered of the coming autumn. It was a beautiful night.

"Look at me, kind one. Would you not have me for your wife?"

Isamu looked. She was clothed only in moonlight, her pale skin glowing like silver. Her shining black hair, unbound and unadorned, fell in dark waves over her shoulders. Her waist and hips formed a perfect curve down to her strong, slender legs. Her arms hung at her sides, long fingers dangling, offering herself unashamed. And above all were her eyes, almond fox-eyes glowing like old gold, like lighthouses in the dark, beckoning him.

He looked away. He did not throw himself at her feet this time, but held his face in his hands. After a while, he looked back up at the moon. To him, it was blurred with tears, surround by a halo of reflected light in beams like delicate spears.

"No," he said.

The fox-maiden made no reply. Isamu felt a desperate need to fill the silence come upon him. "You are beautiful," he said, still gazing at the silver sphere that shone clear in the sky. "Beyond beautiful. Beyond words, beyond anything a human might express, or comprehend. In your gratitude, with your craft, you have given me what I could not have given myself in a thousand lifetimes, and for this I am blessed and thankful.

"I am now," he said matter-of-factly, "the richest man for many miles around. I have money, as you say, and power. If I were to exercise that power in certain ways, I could become a nobleman, a great lord, and my sons would be princes. My house would gain arms and honors, and despite my age I would make a fit husband for any of a thousand noble maidens."

He looked again to the fox-girl. She had chosen to clothe herself, and was wrapped in a wondrous kimono of heartbreaking blue, traced with silver thread that caught the moonlight. Her eyes were wide, her lips trembling.

"But you?" he continued, tears drying on his cheeks as he looked into her liquid eyes. "Never. Never can I marry you. If you have raised me up this high to overcome my shallow objections, I beg you to cast me down again. My true objection cannot be overcome."

He threw himself at her feet then, kneeling before her in the dust and letting his tears burst forth. "Mistress of magic! Honored spirit! Everlasting beauty! You are all a man could want in a woman...but you are not a woman. I will readily admit that I love you. I will even say I worship you. But there it is! I worship you! You are a spirit, a creature of magic, a *kitsune* and a demigod! To marry you, to lay with you, would be an offense, a sin against nature!"

Isamu lay kneeling, face down in the dirt yard of the humble shack that until a few days ago had been all he'd had and he'd wanted. Words poured out of his mouth as tears poured out of his eyes. "I swear in the name of Lord Buddha, O wise one, that my children and my children's children shall honor you as I do, and shall never forget your name and what you have given us. But I cannot do what you ask me to do!"

His forehead was on the ground, his tears making little lakes in the red-brown earth. His eyes were open, and he watched the little rivulets trace their trails in the dirt. The silver light of the moon was everywhere in his narrow field of vision, doubled over as he was. As he knelt, the light seemed to grow stronger, to fill every shadow with its glow, glowing brighter every minute...

Isamu brought himself back up quickly to a kneeling position. Before his eyes, the fox-maiden was shining with silver light, glowing from within. Her face, through the glow, bore a look of transcendental joy. The air was filled with a high, piercing note that continued without pause as the radiance shifted, showing all the colors of the rainbow.

"Kind one!" The fox-maiden's voice was unmistakable, though it rolled like thunder and the glowing figure's mouth did not move. "For 500 years I have searched for the man whose honor and piety could free me from my bondage in animal form. You, Isamu, are that man."

The breeze turned into a wind. The blinding light of the *kitsune* shifted and blurred, sending out glowing beams in all directions. "Know that you have saved me, kind one, that your honor has been my salvation. Take my blessing, and remember me always."

There was a final flash of light, and color and noise—Isamu thought he heard a joyful bark as the glow filled the world—and then there was silence. Nothing was left in the hard-packed yard of the little hut but an old, rich man kneeling in the dirt and weeping with joy.

The Wendigo

"The legend is picturesque enough," observed the doctor after one of the longer pauses, speaking to break it rather than because he had anything to say, "for the Wendigo is simply the Call of the Wild personified, which some natures hear to their own destruction."

"That's about it," Hank said presently. "An' there's no misunderstandin' when you hear it. It calls you by name right enough."

Another pause followed. Then Dr. Cathcart came back to the forbidden subject with a rush that made the others jump.

"The allegory is significant," he remarked, looking about him into the darkness, "for the Voice, they say, resembles all the minor sounds of the Bush—wind, falling water, cries of animals and so forth. And, once the victim hears that—he's off for good, of course..."

—Algernon Blackwood, "The Wendigo"

In the deepest, darkest reaches of North America, from the woods of Minnesota to the primeval forests and wastelands of northern Canada, a savage creature stalks the cold nights. Its cry is the voice of the wild, secret places, and it brings doom to those who hear it, huddled around their flickering fires in the frozen wilderness. In the lore of North American natives, and in the accounts of those tales recorded by European settlers, the creature is known by many names: witiko, atcen, windigo, windigowak *and others. Whatever its name, its blood is ice and it moves* with the wind, driven by an insatiable, maddening hunger for human flesh. It is the Wendigo—and it was once human.

The wendigo is literally a cold-blooded killer, a creature of ice and death. To satisfy its cannibal lust, it kills and eats any man, woman or child it comes across, innocent or guilty. It drives winds and snow before it, howling storms in any season, and the winds carry with them the certain knowledge of death. It's not only isolated woodsmen or travelers who fall victim to this devouring spirit; whole communities may be rendered helpless by the unstoppable wendigo. Where it has passed, it leaves behind only bones, frost and silence.

Its appearance—when it physically appears at all—is as varied as its names. To some, it is a monstrous two-legged beast, huge and hairy, white as the snow. Standing up to 15 feet tall, it has jagged teeth and claws the sickly yellow of old ivory, and it gives off a powerful stench of rot and decay. The wendigo is sometimes described as an immaterial wraith, a howling ghostlike entity that screeches and moans its way through the woods in search of the warm blood that can ease the torment of its cursed existence; or as a towering frost-encrusted skeleton radiating soul-freezing cold, in whose enormous ribcage can be seen a polished lump of brilliant blue ice—the heart of the wendigo. At times, though, the wendigo isn't seen at all, but exists only as a indescribable sound, an unnatural wail that beckons the unwary into the darkness of the wilderness, never to be seen—or, at least, never to be sane—again.

The wendigo is also able, occasionally, to assume an appearance much like its human shape before it was

transformed—though the face will be slack and sunken, the voice empty and babbling, the breath foul and ice-cold, the eyes glowing with sickly red light. But this humanlike form is a shadow, a mockery of the person it once was, a thing to be pitied as much as feared. What happened to bring the victim into the possession of the merciless, eternally starving wendigo spirit or manitou? *What brought down this horrible curse?*

One way people lose their humanity to the wendigo is to hear its eerie cry and be brought under its spell, or even to dream of this happening. It was upon legends of this kind of spiritual attack by the wendigo that Algernon Blackwood based his famous story, "The Wendigo." The howl of the wendigo is irresistible, hypnotic; unless extreme magical measures are taken, those who hear it will be drawn away forever. People taken in this way aren't necessarily trans-formed—although that does happen—but are whisked away with the malicious flesh-eating spirit, flown through the air at the speed of the wind, and drained of their vital essence. Most are gone forever; those few unfortunate vic-tims who escape are destroyed in mind and spirit. Many of these blasted souls descend further and further into mad-ness until bloodlust overtakes them and they become wendigo themselves.

The most common cause for being overtaken by the transforming curse of the wendigo, however, is the breaking of the taboo against eating human flesh. The wendigo spirit doesn't seem to care about the circumstances; the lost and snowbound trapper forced to eat a dead companion to survive is just as cursed as the bloodthirsty warrior who disregards taboo and engages in the savage practice of devouring parts of his slain enemies. It may take an instant or it may take days, but the person who invites possession through this forbidden act will feel his blood running cold, his heart freezing and his soul filling with the wendigo's eternal craving. Transformed into a monster, he is doomed to forever walk the winds and repeat his crime.

Another way that a man may be transformed into a wendigo is to be cursed by a powerful shaman. This act is almost unspeakably evil—only the darkest and most depraved medicine man would bring the unending torment of the wendigo upon someone. To violate the laws of man and nature in this manner is to invite terrible vengeance from the spirits. But it can be done, and according to legend it has been done. Cree artist Carl Ray and folklorist James Stevens recount one such tale in their book, Sacred Legends of the Sandy Lake Cree. *This story of evil, vengeance and redemption also touches on the only sure way of driving out or destroying the wendigo—by melting its heart of ice in the cleansing heat of the sweat lodge or in the purifying flames of a funeral pyre.*

A long time ago, a powerful medicine man named Dark Sky lived at a certain encampment. He was greatly respected, even feared, and as such he was very well-off, having several wives to take care of him and his lodge. But still he wasn't satisfied; there was a certain young woman he greatly desired. He asked the girl's father if he might take her as his wife.

Feared though Dark Sky was, the maiden's father refused the request. Dark Sky was enraged, and went away vowing to bring down powerful medicine against the old man who had insulted him so. He broke camp and moved his lodge and his women and children to another site not far away. That night, he went out into the forest and returned carrying a big ball of snow in two hands. He buried the snowball under the hot ashes of his fire and began to chant an eerie, frenzied song unlike any other. For hours he sang his dark chant, until the snowball had formed a ring of ice. With a forked stick, he held the ice ring to his forehead to complete the ritual.

At that moment, the air was ripped apart by sudden howling winds. Trees lashed back and forth like whips, and freezing gusts tore across the land, bringing driving snow with them. Echoing within the screams of the wind were the screams of terrified people. The evil Dark Sky smiled with grim satisfaction; he knew that the wendigo spirit had possessed the girl he'd been refused. He had heard the death screams of her family and friends on the wind, and knew her camp was no more. He returned to the cursed encampment, which was blood-soaked and littered with gnawed bones, to retrieve his prize: the wendigo-woman.

Because he'd created her, he could control her, and with his magic he led the she-monster back to his camp. There he erected a special tent with a heap of heated rocks in its center, and placed the possessed creature within it. The wendigo began to sweat great amounts of water as the ice that had blighted the girl's spirit began to melt and pour out of her body. For a whole day the she-thing was roasted in the sweat lodge, until at last there was nothing left of the wendigo and the beautiful maiden lay there, human once again.

Dark Sky took the girl into his household as his wife. She was his favorite, not only because she was youngest and prettiest, but because he had won her with the powerful black medicine of which he was so proud. But none of the evil medicine man's other wives would accept her. They wouldn't even talk to her—wouldn't even *look* at her—unless there was no way it could be avoided. She was lonely and confused, having no memory of the twisted way in which she'd been used. Again and again she pestered her husband to tell her what was the matter, and finally he relented. Angrily, he told her what had been done to her, and what she had done while possessed by the wendigo he'd summoned.

The girl was completely shattered to learn of the great evil she'd been induced to commit under the control of the wendigo-spirit. There was no one she could turn to, nowhere to run—her family and people were dead by her cursed hand, consumed by the eternal hunger of the wendigo, and still she was utterly shunned by Dark Sky's other wives. Even the diabolical old shaman had ceased to speak to her, having turned his fickle attentions to another of his women. She was completely forsaken.

As the long, lonely days passed, the woman felt a chill growing in her bones. Even near a cheerful cookfire or under the life-giving light of *geesis*, the sun, she could not get warm. The girl knew exactly what was happening: the wendigo spirit was taking her again. As all things come around in circles, the Great Spirit would use her to punish Dark Sky for his unforgivable crimes. With each day and night, she felt the ice forming again in her bones, felt her heart freezing, felt the first horrible cravings for the hot human blood that might, for a time, relieve the unending chill.

At last, the evening came when she knew she would be human no longer. She sat, alone as usual, listening to the day's end sounds of the evil sorcerer's camp, feeling her heart slowly freeze and harden. The wendigo spirit inside her cried for blood and revenge. But she could hear the women gossiping and singing, could hear the children playing and crying; though they'd shunned her, these people were innocent of Dark Sky's sins. They didn't deserve the gruesome, screaming death the wendigo would visit upon the camp.

As a sudden, bitter wind began to whip through the trees and the frost closed over her soul, the young woman picked up a sharp knife and brought it to her breast. She died human, cold tears on her cheeks.

Two Barrels of Silver

It wouldn't be right to publish a collection called Werewolves and Shapeshifters *without including at least one story in which the shapeshifter in question is a full-on, claws-'n'-fangs Hollywood werewolf, a monster whose only job is to scare people, spill blood and die, after a spectacular fight, by a silver bullet right where it counts. This is that story, but of course I couldn't make it that simple.*

This story is based on a story from the German city of Greifswald, from the 17th century. It involved a gang of werewolves that terrorized the town from their base on a street called Rokoverstrasse. Some young bucks decided they'd had enough of these wolf-men rampaging through the town at will, and decided to strike back. After their first assault, they got thoroughly romped. But they went back a second time, having melted down all their buckles, buttons and medals into werewolf-killing silver bullets, and cleaned house. Perfect Hollywood story structure.

After working on it for a while, I realized I didn't have the time, or the desire, to write a story set in 17th-century Germany. I already had a story set in 17th-century France, and I needed something, well, cooler. *So I started playing around. For a while, the heroes were high-school football players, and the werewolf boss was some kind of drug dealer. Then the heroes became some trailer-park good ol' boys—and the boss monster was still a drug dealer. I was stuck and unhappy.*

Then, while spending Christmas with at my brother's place, I happened to catch Young Guns *on satellite TV. The combination of Emilio Estevez and the wide-open spaces of southern Alberta just clicked, and "Two Barrels of Silver" was born. It just* made sense *to have werewolves in the mythical Old West. People bring their cultures with them when they migrate, and with cultures come monsters. The West was opened because people wanted room to live, and fresh opportunities—who's to say that werewolves, so long pushed into the shadows by fearful, crowding, humans, wouldn't want a part of that?*

In the end, though, it was just plain old fun to write a pulp Western adventure story, and have cowboys fight werewolves. I hope you enjoy reading it as much as I did writing it.

The bunkhouse door burst inward, admitting the slash of rain, the howl of wind and two bleeding men, one staggering under the supported weight of the other.

"Ellie, fetch bandages and water!" Sam McKenna shouted through a split lip; the left side of his face was a bruised mass, raked by a half-dozen deep cuts. "Kurt's banged up bad!"

McKenna shrugged the dead weight of the unconscious man down onto nearest cot, rainwater and red blood soaking into the rough canvas, and slumped exhausted against the log wall. He hooked the plank door shut with one boot heel as Eleanor Lucas rushed over from the bunkhouse stove, basin and bandages in hand.

"Lord, Sam! What happened?" cried the pretty redhead as she knelt and bent over the still body on the bunk, practiced hands moving to peel away layers of blood-soaked cloth and leather.

"Later, El, later," McKenna drawled, weary. "You just tend to Kurt, and let me catch my own breath." The bearded blond ranch foreman pulled a battered flask from inside his rain-heavy leather overcoat, unscrewed the rattling cap and took a deep pull. Strong golden whiskey mixed with matted red blood in his beard; he drank the last drop and let the flask clatter to the wooden floor.

What happened?

Sheesh, what *didn't* happen? And where do you start to tell about it? Maybe you start with the dead cattle, dozens of them, torn up and left where they lay. "Wolves," they said, because there was nothing else to say. But there's never been a wolf that didn't take everything he could get, or take the best bits and leave some meat behind. There's never been a wolf that killed for the hell of it.

You could start with the stagecoach massacre, with half-eaten horses, passenger and driver—him still holding a shotgun that hadn't fired a shot. "Wolves," they said, because there was nothing else to say. But there's never been a wolf that gave two hoots about a lady's jewelry or a man's money or a case of good liquor. And there's never been a mad-dog stage robber that wouldn't take a dead man's gun.

And then there's the sheriff, a big man out of John Neuman's Tumbling 'T' spread, who says "wolves" every time some dumb animal's found dead with nothing but her udders missing, who says "wolves" every time a coachman loses his throat before he can fire a shot, who says "wolves" when Boss Lucas (*Lord, rest his soul!*) turns up dead on his own doorstep missing a few of his parts and most of his blood.

If you were of a certain frame of mind, you might make mention of the Tumbling 'T' hands who all of a sudden have pretty necklaces to give to their favorite women, of Neuman men flashing money they never could've earned in two lazy, drunken lifetimes. Maybe you'd start your story with a county in the grip of fear.

Or maybe you'd start with a bunch of good ol' Lucas boys—himself, his brother David, "Doc" Larsen and nine-odd others—who figured they knew where Hell was being raised, who figured they could gear up and bring it all down...

...*a bunch of dumb cowpunchers who didn't know how wrong they were.*

McKenna's bitter train of thought was interrupted by a sharp gasp from the young woman working on his man. He glanced over to see her staring down at Kurt Muller's ravaged chest, a tatter of red-stained coat in each hand, eyes wide with shock.

"Sam, he...he hasn't been shot," she said, disbelief in her voice.

McKenna turned away, staring out into the distance beyond the bunkhouse walls. "No, I don't suppose he has."

"It looks he was attacked by, by a dog or a...oh my God. Oh, Jesus, Sam...Doc was right, wasn't he? About Neuman and his gang?"

"You mean, how they're wolves that can pass for men, or maybe the other way around? Yeah, he was right, but I don't figure he was too happy when he got his proof. He was the first one to get it, right as we rode up just about sundown. Ambush. Didn't even get to scream, 'cause he didn't have a throat left to scream with."

His voice cracked, and he reached for his dropped flask, tilting it back and throwing it against the far wall when he found it empty.

"Oh, Ellie, it was...I mean, they were all over us! We never had a chance against those things. Some of 'em went on four legs, and some went on two, but they were all fast as devils. I don't even know how many there were. After Doc went down they got Vernon, pulled him right out of the saddle and tossed him a good 20 yards into the side of an old woodshed. He never got up."

McKenna was almost sobbing now, his hands shaking as he sketched the battle with gestures in the air. "We opened up on them, shooting point blank, and it was like they didn't even feel it. I put a big helping of buckshot into the back of one of them...them things, one who was ripping into Brassard, and it was like its body just ate the lead right up. No blood, nothing. There was nothing we could do!"

The bearded cowboy buried his face in his hands, scrubbing at his eyes with calloused fingers as if to tear away the vision of the slaughter at the Tumbling 'T'. Ellie knelt, frozen with fear—she'd never known the tough-as-nails foreman to lose his composure like this, and the sight terrified her. At last he spoke again, his voice flat and tight.

"When Campbell went down shooting, I hollered for the rest of the boys to make a run for it. We were done for, Ellie. We all scattered, like we'd planned, going different ways so they couldn't chase all of us. I think maybe five out of the dozen of us got away—or were allowed to escape. If those things had wanted us dead, I know they would've been fast enough to catch us all.

"But I heard 'em howling and laughing as we high-tailed it out of there, laughing just like you'd imagine a dog would laugh. I came back as the crow flies, 'cause I'd picked up Kurt. He'd lost his horse, but he was still breathing, so I..."

McKenna swung his head up sharply, snapping out of his story, and looked from the unmoving body of his friend on the bench to the pale-faced young woman. Trembling, she gave her head a tight shake.

"Ah, damnit. Bring me the bottle, would you? And cover his face." Eleanor did so, and McKenna took a long, hard pull of the amber liquid. He looked up at the girl, studying her face for a second before passing the bottle up to her. She took it and matched his man-sized swig.

She's a Lucas, all right, McKenna thought, almost smiling. Old George never had any sons, and Mrs. Lucas passed on when Ellie was just little, so the girl had been raised pretty rough 'n' tumble. A real rancher's daughter, if ever there was one.

"El, you're a good girl," he said, fumbling for the right words. "You shouldn't have any part of what's coming. We're all marked men. Neuman, whatever he is, knows us and knows we know him, and he'll have us all eventually. Every Lucas man is just as dead as Kurt over there. Get out of here, girl. Take what you can and run, go East, get as far from this damned place as you can!"

White-faced and shivering, Eleanor Lucas struggled to keep her tears under control as she met McKenna's eyes and held them. "Sam McKenna," she began, breathing in tight little gasps, "this is my Daddy's land—my land now—and I don't intend to leave it. And...and I don't intend to leave *you!* You can't make me!"

McKenna, still sitting propped against the wall by the door, where he'd first thrown himself, looked up into the tear-filled eyes of the fiery young redhead. Wood cracked and spit in the stove; the storm howled outside.

"No," he said after a long while. "No, I guess I can't."

There came a sudden hammering at the door. McKenna's Colt revolver was out of its leather before the second pounding knock had landed, and Eleanor stumbled backward, clapping a hand to her mouth to muffle a scream. The pair waited, barely breathing, until the knocking came again.

"McKenna! McKenna, let us in, damnit!" It was Dale Kitt's voice, the short-tempered cowboy's unmistakable rapid-fire voice barely muffled by the door's thick planks. The relieved foreman holstered his weapon and slapped open the heavy latch, and two muddy and rain-soaked men tumbled into the warmth and light of the Lucas bunkhouse.

Kitt was first through the door, swearing and cursing in a running stream of profanity as he shook cascades of rainwater from his hat and clothing. A compact but tough little rooster of a man, he was the newest hand on the ranch, having been brought on just the season before. Dark-haired and dark-eyed, fast-talking and fast-moving, he was tightlipped about only one subject—his own past, what he did and who he was before signing on with Boss Lucas. But capable help was scarce in those parts and he had an easy way with animals; if the man wanted to keep the stories of his scars to himself, that was his own business.

Close on Kitt's heels came young Jason Quinney, who was in most ways the exact opposite of the older man. Lanky, fair-haired and smooth-faced, Quinney was quiet and unobtrusive, watching and absorbing everything around him with startling gray eyes; when he spoke he spoke carefully, in the broad tones of his native New England. He'd claimed to be 17 years old when he first arrived looking for work, but even three years later nobody could mistake him for being a day over 18. He'd had more schooling than most of the other hands, and Doc Larsen had taken him under his wing. A quick study and an earnest worker, the kid was on his way to being a fine cattleman. But his icy eyes were wide with shock now, his baby face bone-white as he shut and latched the door against the horrors of the stormy night.

"Damnit, Sam!" Kitt wasted no time in getting a rant going, channeling his adrenaline into his temper. "What the hell? I mean, *what the hell?* What happened out there, man? That was damned slaughter! I didn't sign up for this craziness! Rustlers, horse thieves, stage robbers, bandits, Indians? Fine. Monster-men ripping fellas' throats out and eating bullets like beans? Forget it. Far as I'm concerned, this damn ranch, this whole lunatic county, can go straight to..."

The tirade broke off abruptly as the raging cowboy's eyes registered for the first time the ragged corpse on the cot nearest the door. The fight went out of his brawler's body, his set jaw went slack. The iron tang of blood was in the air. "Ah, hell," he said quietly, with a little laugh like a sob. "Kurt too?"

Kitt let himself drop into a rough wooden chair, sprawling, deflated; the big-hearted German had been well-liked by the whole crew. He caught the bottle McKenna tossed his way and downed a wicked swig, his cold-coffee eyes still fixed on Muller's body. He absently passed the dwindling container of whiskey up to the silent youth who still stood by his side. As if waking from a dream, Quinney took a draught of the fiery liquid, wincing slightly as he swallowed; drinking hard liquor was the only important cowboy skill he'd been slow to pick up.

"What are we...what do we do now, Sam?" the young man asked, passing the bottle back with shaking hands.

Now that his hands—a couple of them, at least—were here, the despair and uncertainty was gone from McKenna's voice, replaced by the rawhide and boot-leather needed to boss rough men. "Well, before we talk about what we're going to do," he began, "we'd better get an idea of our own situation. First, it's damned good to see you both in one piece, fellas. Now, many others made it out of that mess? I saw Brassard go down, and Campbell, Vernon and...and Doc. Sorry, kid."

"At least he...at least he went out doing what he...loved best—b-being right," Quinney replied with an attempt at a smile. McKenna attempted to smile back. Behind them, Eleanor had begun wrapping Kurt's body. The rustling of the blankets was the sound of Death's wings.

"I guess you're right, at that." McKenna stared up through the ceiling, cradling the bottle. "Wolf-men! Werewolves! I thought he'd finally read one book too many. If only I'd..." He broke off and put the steel back in his voice. "Well, 'if only' nothing...we've got a problem, so let's deal with it. Did Nugent make it?"

Kitt shook his head. "No, sir. Ol' Ted finally met the animal he couldn't kill. I saw him go down after his horse threw him. Died with a knife in his hand."

Damn, McKenna thought. *He was a good shot.* He laughed inwardly, bitterly, then. *What good is a sharp-shooter if bullets are worthless?*

Kitt was still talking rapidly, counting off Lucas hands on his dirty fingers. "Buckle likely got out; I saw him high-tailin' it north. I figure that half-breed's playing it smart, making for Indian territory."

McKenna nodded. "Dwayne Buckle can take care of himself, all right. I figure he'll make it; the Devil himself could scarce catch that Cheyenne pony of his."

Kitt finished another big pull of the whiskey that had found its way back to his hands. "'Course, the Devil might be just who we're messin' with. We got any more of this here juice, Miss Lucas?"

Quinney spoke up as the dark-haired man tried to shake the last precious drops from the empty bottle. "F-Frank made it too. I mean, I think he made it. Before it got too dark to see, we...well, I saw him about a half-mile away, riding almost as we were. If he's not...not lost in the storm, he should be getting here fairly soon."

That was good news; Frank Grill was as solid as they come. But McKenna's stomach was a cold knot; he dreaded the last, obvious question because he dreaded the answer. Searching his men's eyes, he asked simply, "David?"

The two hands looked at each other, then back to the foreman. "I don't know, Sam," Kitt began. "I just don't rightly know.

"Last I saw of your brother, me and the kid were already saying a speedy goodbye to the goddamn Tumblin' 'T'." The wiry horseman gazed longingly into the depths of the empty bottle.

"He was still mounted, headed 'round back of the ranch house, riding hard. Maybe making for the creek, trying to cut his trail. Creek'd be running pretty high with these rains we've been havin', but his Queenie's a sure-footed old nag. If any horse's gonna find a way across a swollen creek, it'll be her."

McKenna nodded; he could feel Ellie's worrying eyes on him. "Thanks, Dale. I guess that's as good o' news as I could've expected. We've gotta hope for the best."

"Hey, now *that's* a good plan, boss!" Kitt was feeling the whiskey and getting his temper back. "'Hope for the best,' he says! And what do you figure I should be hoping for, *exactly?* Huh? What's the best that"—he stopped to count on his fingers—"*three,* maybe six, fellas can hope for against a bloodthirsty gang of goddamn seven-foot-tall cannibal *wolf-men?* Goddamnit!"

The bottle shattered against the door to McKenna's right, sending a cascade of tinkling glass shrapnel to the floor. The silence that followed was deadly, the foreman glaring up at the red-faced ranchhand. Wearily, he pulled himself up off the bunkhouse floor and began slowly crossing the length of room. Kitt scrambled to his feet, knowing he'd gone too far, ready to fight.

But the blond-bearded cowboy walked right past him, boots and spurs loud as gunshots in the quiet tension of the bunkhouse, and went to his own footlocker.

"First things first," he said without turning, flicking the lid of the chest open with the toe of his boot. "Kid, take Kurt outside and bury him shallow. We'll put him in the ground proper in the morning." He bent down and pulled a full bottle of whiskey from the locker, broke the seal, took a savage pull and slapped the cork back in.

"As for what else we're gonna do..." McKenna whirled around, whipping the bottle overhand at Kitt, who caught it one-handed with a fighter's reflexes. The slap of glass on Kitt's leathery palm was a whipcrack over Eleanor's startled gasp.

"...why don't we start by drinking to my brother's health?"

He'd worked at his bonds for a good quarter-hour, as best he could figure, and all he had to show for it was deeper burns on his wrists, aching arms and shoulders, and rough ropes that seemed tighter than when he'd started. *Gotta save my strength*, thought David McKenna, not for the first time. *Never know when I'll get the chance to bust out of here.*

That chance seemed remote. He was tied hand and foot to a straight-backed chair, and that chair was hanging some distance off the floor of a darkened barn. He could tell it was a barn by the smell, though there was no sound of animals other than the grotesquely half-human growls and barks coming from the yard outside; livestock didn't last long around this bunch, he guessed. It was still some time before dawn, so aside from the odd red glimmer from the wolves' bonfire, no light leaked into the barn. The rain still hadn't let up, though, so plenty of water did; he was drenched, swinging in the stinking darkness of John Neuman's empty horse barn, waiting for Fate to play its hand.

It'd sure been a raw deal, so far. He and his older brother had gone vigilante on the corrupt murderers of the Tumbling 'T', along with the Lucas hands that'd had the guts to stick around after the Boss turned up dead. Now, a lot of those same guts had been spilled all over the hard-packed yard out there. McKenna doubted they'd stayed spilled for long, though; by the stomach-turning sounds of animal feasting that'd reached him through the worn walls of the barn, Neuman's gang—or pack?—ate every morsel. If he lived through this, he had a new and literal definition of "mad-dog killer."

Rope and rafters creaked as he hung there listening to the savage festivities outside, thinking of how close he'd come to making it out of this madhouse. If only he'd made it to the creek...but Queenie, already near panic from the smell of the wolf-men, had been whipped an inch too far and had stumbled, screaming, throwing him hard. His head said hello to a tree stump, and the next thing he knew he was here, trussed like a turkey.

A sound of scrabbling on wood came from over to McKenna's right, in the direction of his slow rotation. The big barn door was being pulled open, and as it came into his field of vision he made out two figures silhouetted against the glow of the firelight, one man-shaped, the other the all-too-familiar form of a nightmare made real.

The man carried with him the faint glow of a trimmed-down oil lamp.

John Neuman's voice, lower-pitched and rougher than when McKenna had heard it last but still bearing a hint of German accent, came up through the half-darkness. It sounded like he was talking with his mouth full.

"Lower him. Not all the way."

The hulking figure at the rancher's side moved into the shadows, and McKenna felt himself being lowered in rough jerks toward the ground. Soon he and his chair were hanging with his boots maybe three feet off the floor.

"Leave us."

The bulk of the wolf-man was seen once more before the big door swung shut and the barn dipped again into darkness. McKenna watched the faint glow approach, heard the lantern set down on a wooden milking stool. In a rattle of brass and glass, the flame blossomed. The young cowboy was rotating in the center of the sphere of light, surrounded by a lattice of timbers and shadow. John Neuman was before him, walking slowly, keeping pace with McKenna's slow spin. He looked more or less human now, but there was still something animal to his looks, something that suggested a dog's muzzle rather than a man's face. In his hand was a battered camp plate, and from it the rancher plucked a small piece of meat, cooked but very rare. McKenna's mouth watered involuntarily—it must have been over half a day since he'd eaten.

Neuman popped the morsel into his mouth and chewed slowly, with theatrical relish, as McKenna spun and glared. Their gradual turn brought them back to the milking stool and the lamp, and the German bent to place the plate on the ground. He stood, making a show of licking his fingers, and stopped McKenna's spin with one bare foot.

The murderous cattleman, with one last smacking suck of his thumb, grinned at his captive. McKenna watched the two long fangs retract, and the animalistic characteristics of the face melt into the features of a normal, even jolly-looking man somewhere beyond middle age.

"Hello, young mister McKenna." The beast-man's voice had risen two octaves to its normal pitch and precise European smoothness. He wore a pinstriped vest over his bare chest.

"Neuman." McKenna refused to look away from those pale blue predator's eyes.

"I apologize for not offering you some refreshment," the rancher continued, brightly, glancing down at the grease-stained plate by his feet. "I fear you wouldn't care for the table I set."

The smiling German winked, and leaned in close for a stage whisper. "It doesn't taste *anything* like chicken, by the way."

McKenna would have spit, if his mouth hadn't been bone-dry. "What do you want from me, Neuman? Why am I in a chair instead of on a plate?"

"Ah, the eternal question. 'Why am I here?' I knew you were smarter than your brother, but I didn't know you were a philosopher too." He grinned sadistically.

"But, to answer your question, I'm afraid I must admit that your presence here is a somewhat of a matter of ego—mine, of course. You see, my people out there are rather...*unrefined*. Even when they were men—those that ever were men—they weren't given to sensitive thinking. Now...well, you see them for yourself; they have a lot of growing up to do. They can't yet truly appreciate the exquisite irony and historic significance of what I'm accomplishing in this territory. But *you* can. And you *will*, before we're through.

"In short, David, you are here so that I may have the delicious, selfish pleasure of gloating."

"Gloating over what? A pile of dead bodies and a big chunk of empty range for your dogs to run on? What *are* you, Neuman?"

McKenna could smell Neuman's graveyard breath as he stepped in close, smiling, to whisper: "What do you think I am?"

"A monster."

The smile broadened into a wolf's grin. "I thought you might say that."

Neuman's fist flashed out, exploding into McKenna's face with a crunch of bone and sending the bound man flying backward on his rope tether. McKenna was swinging again, seeing stars, the room spinning around him as a trail of blood from his shattered nose made looping designs in the dust of the barn's floor.

"Because that's what your kind always says! What you've been saying for 10,000 years!" Neuman was shouting now, his powerful voice shading back into its animal tones.

"Monsters, devils, demons, vampires! Things to be hated, hunted, driven out! For millennia you've pushed us back from your ever-widening circle of firelight, torch-light, lamplight. Back to woods cleared of trees, hills mined bare, valleys choked with the stinking refuse of your millions, your *billions*. You're a plague, a mindless disease! For you, there can never be enough, so you build machines, guns, factories...anything to get *more*, to expand yourselves beyond what the earth can willingly bear."

The aristocratic man-wolf had regained some of his composure, but not his wholly human form. The arc of McKenna's pendulum had settled down to a gentle pace, and the young cattleman could see his captor clearly. The man's brows had thickened, the widow's peak of his hair-line dropping nearly to the bridge of his nose. His nose itself had broadened and flattened, reaching down to form a snarling muzzle with his jutting jaws, elongated teeth and tightened lips. His face had gained three days' growth of beard in three minutes, and the graying hair was the color of dusty brick. His eyes were ice.

McKenna knew he was seeing the creature's true face.

Neuman continued his lecture, pacing around the bound man as he swung; McKenna was reminded of Doc Larsen, the unlucky old know-it-all. "But we are were-wolves," the wolf-man said, with a growling note of pride. "We are creatures of the earth and children of the moon. We won't take what the earth won't give. We need wild spaces to roam and game to hunt. But even in crowded old Europe, crushed under the weight of mankind, there are still untouched places to be found. And for those of us who can tolerate them, even your teeming ant-hill cities can be a wilderness of sorts, where we hunt a different sort of game. Yes, even in Europe, despite your best efforts, we survive. We are few—precious few, and far between—but we survive."

Neuman reached up and grabbed the rope that suspended the chair, once again stopping McKenna's slow rocking. The aching of the cowboy's body was beginning to trump the pain of his broken nose. Neuman leaned in close again, dropping his voice to a menacing rumble.

"Survive, yes." His wolf-eyes searched the man's face. "But we are—some of us, anyway—thinking, feeling creatures. For what thinking being is mere survival enough? To skulk, to scrabble, to hide in the shadows and live off leavings and remnants like parasites—no, it's not enough to survive. We must thrive!"

He was pacing again now, with triumph in his voice. "And *that*, my dear mister McKenna, is what I'm here for. *This* is what I am: a prophet for my people, a Moses, a Messiah. I will lead them out of bondage to the promised land—*here*. You think this great New West, these open expanses of grass and forest and hills and mountains, is the future of your race? Think again, human. Here, it is you who are weak and fearful, scattered thinly, or huddled in pathetic villages, just like the old days. This is wilderness, lawless and free, and it's here we will at last carve out a new land for ourselves, our own realm free from the cancer of your machine-worship—a kingdom of wolves!"

McKenna's blood ran cold, as much as it *could* run given the ropes cutting off his circulation. He'd heard his share of hellfire preachers before, and Neuman had that frighteningly clear tone of a real True Believer—dangerous and crazy. The taste of blood was in the cowboy's mouth, his face a throbbing mass of pain. Still, he thought, if only he could keep this crazy wolf-man talking long enough, maybe Sam could...

No way. Even if Sam's still alive, there's no way he could do anything to these dogs. Whatever happens, I'm a goner.

But, still, he had to try. "Hey, Neuman...if your numbers are so few, how're you plannin' on..."

Neuman coughed, or barked, sharply and held up one leather-palmed hand, cutting off his prisoner's question. "Excuse me," he growled in a tight, almost choking, voice.

The man in the suspended chair watched as the wolf-man's face contorted, his hairy neck rolling and turning, the muscle and bone of his body seeming to shift and flow as he writhed, eyes closed but still standing. He acted like a man who'd just swallowed a big gulp of hot coffee, fresh off the fire. At last, he there came a rumbling sound from the werewolf's throat, and with a ragged *hawwwk* he raised his head and flicked it forward, spitting into the dirt.

McKenna looked down. Instead of spit, there lay on the floor a heavy lead slug, a .38 by the look of it, deformed by impact on bone. Neuman reached down and picked it up between two clawed fingers, examined it casually.

"Ah! I thought there might be one more left. These big fellows can take time working their way out." He tossed the slug away, and it clattered in the darkness beyond the lamplight. "I'm sorry. You were saying?"

The bullet reminded McKenna of just how tough these monsters were, unkillable with the tools normally used to kill things. Maybe Neuman wasn't crazy. Maybe he could pull it off, slaughter himself an empire of beast-men on the open range. The horror of it made his skin crawl.

But he had to keep talking; every minute of life was another minute of gamblers' hope. "I was sayin', how do you figure you can take all this land? Sounds like you and your precious few buddies might be spreading yourselves pretty thin."

"I'm glad you asked that!" Neuman gave a barking little giggle; his grin was a picket fence of gleaming teeth. *No, he's definitely crazy.* "It so happens this is a matter of personal pride for me. You see, I'm not just a prophet, but a missionary. Only I convert bodies as well as souls.

"I am 400 years old, David. In that time I've gone from being less than a beast to being more than a man. I've reconciled my nature, mastered my transformations, and in so doing I've learned secrets, the deepest secrets of my kind. The whispered curses of the mystical Romany of the Balkans, the spells and charms of dreaming Egypt and ancient Asia, the midnight rituals of my own native Black Forest. I am the Werewolf Lord, human, and I make men over in my image."

McKenna spat blood at the deranged man-monster's feet. "Whether they like it or not, huh?"

Neuman's tone brightened. "Oh, you'd be surprised! Your kind worships violence; the gun is your god. Show a man that his god is powerless—as I have shown you and the other Lucas lackeys—and he soon sees the light, the power that I offer. Just ask your good sheriff and his deputies out there. Or look at yourself! Were you one of us, your blood would have stopped flowing before it could ruin that lovely buckskin coat of yours. More likely, your nose wouldn't have broken at all. Those ropes certainly wouldn't have been enough to keep you bound."

The werewolf was pacing again, and as he walked behind McKenna he gave the hanging chair an idle shove, setting it in motion once again.

"But magic is an art, not a science. It is, as you might say, somewhat of a crap shoot. I can load the dice to a significant degree, but every human responds differently. An upright judge, a pillar of his community, may emerge as a nearly mindless animal, all instinct and blood-thirst, while an illiterate thug may be created nearly as advanced as I, his mind intact and his will stronger than the transforming pull of the moon. All will have their place in my new dominion, from shock troopers to generals, slaves to governors.

"Some, of course, will have a more...*fundamental* role to play." An evil smile twisting his half-human face, Neuman inclined his head toward the greasy plate beside the stool.

"Yeah? So where does that leave me?" The rope creaked like the lid of a cheap coffin.

"Excellent! We return to our original question!" The wolf-man clasped his hands, steepling two clawed fingers at his black lips and taking on a thoughtful tone. "Until now you've been a special case, David, but I'm afraid that here, in the end, your fate boils down to that of all men— do I kill you or convert you?" Those cold wolf-eyes ran over him like he was a bull at auction.

"And?"

"And it all depends, David, on whether I'm bored...or hungry."

"All right, kid. Tell us how we're gonna take care of these things." Sam McKenna sat with his coffee in his hands, looking even more tired and sad-eyed than usual; not only had he just buried a good man, he was also powerfully hung over. He and Dale Kitt had spent the night with the bottle, joined eventually—thankfully—by big Frank Grill, while Quinney had ransacked Doc's books and notes for some dealing with Neuman and his pack of wolf-men.

The slender youth cleared his throat and fidgeted with the few pages of notes he held. It had been a long night for him too. It was bad enough that he'd been working in a near panic, expecting at any moment a huge, furry claw to come smashing through the ranch house window and take a chunk out of his throat. It was worse that every turn of a page had reminded him of his murdered friend, a man who'd treated him like a son.

He looked down at the notes in his hand, the pages crammed with Doc's tidy, tiny, impeccably neat handwriting. The old guy (*How old had he really been, anyway?*) hadn't really been a cattle man, any more than he'd been a bona fide medical doctor, or anything else in particular—he had stories of wild storms at sea, of turbaned bandits on the Silk Road, of teeming African jungles and beautiful Russian girls. Maybe all of it was true, maybe none of it was. But he could ride and rope and handle himself in a scrape, and the Lucas spread was where his road had taken him. Maybe this wasn't his home, but it was home enough that he'd had his library, three big steamer trunks of books—shipped here and proudly installed in the main house.

He knew! He was right, and we laughed. We laughed so hard we had him laughing at his own self. But he was right! He knew, and we...

The tink-tink-tink of Kitt's tapping on his tin coffee cup brought Quinney back to reality. He'd been halfway to nodding off.

"Kid, you sure Doc didn't keep a bottle in his desk?" Even the dark-eyed cowboy's teasing had a fatigued, half-hearted tone. "Your eyes look like two pee-holes in a snowbank."

"Uh...sorry. I got to thinking..." Quinney took a quick, noisy, sip from his own steaming cup, to interrupt himself. "Anyway. Doc had a lot of strange stuff in there, books of legends, stories and...well, I guess we can't call them myths anymore, can we?"

His desperate joke was swallowed by the impatient, hungover silence of the room.

"Right. As far as I can figure, then, there are three ways we might be able to handle these things, and none of them are real good news." His voice was falling into an unconscious imitation of Doc's schoolteacher cadence. "The first one depends on what kind of werewolf we're dealing with. Since Neuman's German—or at least Germanic—there's a good chance he's got a talisman of some kind that's the key to his..."

"A tally-*what*?" Frank Grill knew wrangling and wrestling, and that was about it.

"A talisman, like a magic charm. In this case usually a wolfskin belt or girdle, maybe even a whole pelt, that holds the transformation power. It's like a part of the thing's body. Get hold of it, and you've got your wolf-man by the short hairs. Destroy it, and he's a goner."

Dale Kitt spoke up from where he lay on the bunk he'd gone back to, his voice muffled by the battered hat that covered his face. "Just like that, huh? Well, what are we waitin' for? Let's just go and ask polite for his magic belt."

"Hey, I *said* it isn't looking pretty. I'm just telling you what I got from Doc's notes. If you don't want to..."

Sam held up a weary hand. "Easy, kid, easy. Go on an' show us the second ugly whore we get to choose from."

Quinney blushed and looked nervously over at Eleanor, who was sitting on a the chair by the stove. If he needed an indication of how close to breaking they all were, McKenna's crude talk was it; ordinarily, if a lady was present, Sam wouldn't say "horse manure" if his mouth was full of it.

"Uh...right." He cleared his throat again. "The second one's not much better looki...er, not much better. There's a plant called aconite, what folks call 'monkshood' or 'wolfsbane.' Real pretty too, but deadly as hell. For normal people it's a fairly nasty poison, but for werewolves it's pure snakebite. They can't even go near it; I guess the smell alone is enough to make em' toss their biscuits."

"Lemme guess. This stuff only grows in China, right?"

"Yeah, it grows in China, Frank. And in England, and France, and Germany and all over the place back East."

"Just not in these parts, huh?" Sam's grin was bitter. "Way our luck's runnin', I guess we oughtta be thankful we're fightin' monsters instead of gambling."

"Well, apparently it does grow around here, but it's not very common. This is the edge of its range; aconite likes it cooler and wetter than we normally get. Could probably find some in sheltered spots, gullies and creeks and the like. Maybe. Doc never got around to figuring that part out."

"And I sure as hell don't want to be flower-picking all over God's green earth with a pack of wolf-men waiting to play fox-and-hounds with me." Only Kitt's hat moved; the cowboy himself was still sprawled motionless. Quinney had assumed he was asleep.

"Damn, I wish Buckle was here," Sam cursed. Frank had confirmed that the half-breed had been making for Indian territory after the disaster at the Tumbling 'T'. "Ol' Dwayne knows how to find every useful thing that comes up out of the ground."

"Huh. Well, maybe he's just gone for supplies, then," Kitt muttered. "Gonna borrow us a bushel of wolf-man poison from those redskins o' his."

Sam ignored him. "All right, kid. Do I even want to hear what's next?"

Quinney shrugged. "Depends, Sam. You're not a millionaire banker, are you?"

"What d'you mean by that?"

"I mean, all we need is a few pounds of silver."

"Oh, is that all? A few pounds? Why didn't you say so? I got plenty up at my mansion."

"Yeah, well, I wish you did. It's the sure-fire way to take out werewolves, I guess. Silver bullets, silver blades—it don't matter how you do it, as long as it's silver. They call it the metal of the moon, and the moon is the only thing that has power over these things. It cuts them, burns them—one shot, apparently, and *poof*. Goodbye shaggy dog."

Eleanor spoke up, her voice cracking slightly. "What about...well, what about my...my mother's silverware? Do you suppose we could melt it down and..."

Kitt's voice cut her off abruptly. "Don't you dare touch a single one of your mama's teaspoons, Miss Lucas." All eyes turned to the tough little man, sitting bolt upright on his bunk. He looked like he didn't know whether to laugh or cry.

"We're saved, boys. Damn me to hell for wishing it could have been any other way, but we're saved. Ol' Dale's gonna set you up with enough pure silver to plug an *army* of wolf-men."

"What the hell are you talking about, Dale?" Sam glared over his bushy blond moustache. "You still drunk, or what?"

Kitt made a face like he'd swallowed bitter medicine. He looked down at the ground, hat in hands, scuffing at the floorboards with the toe of one boot.

"Aww...hell, boys. I don't have to paint you a picture, do I? Let's just say it involves a certain train, and a certain bunch of fellers and a certain other bunch of fellers that're real anxious to fit yours truly with a fancy new necktie two sizes too tight."

"Well, I'll be damned..." Quinney spoke for the everybody in the room.

"Put your eyes back in your head, kid. Look, I'm sorry I ain't been straight with you boys. 'Specially you, Sam. But I've got the payroll of Judas cached in a coulee 'bout six miles down-country, a small stash of silver that's gonna save our sorry behinds."

"Train robber, huh?" Sam cocked an eye at the dark-haired man. "Laying low until the heat's off."

"Honest, Sam, I ain't like that no more. I scored big and barely made it out with my skin, and I'm through with robbin' folks. I'm a cattleman now, and probably always will be, especially if you all get too trigger-happy when we hit the Tumbling 'T'."

"All right then." Sam stood to shake the bandit-turned-cowboy's hand. "I guess we're all in this together, anyhow."

"Thanks, boss," Kitt grinned. "Frank, you wanna ride out with me?"

Frank Grill was out of his chair with a slap of big palms on powerful thighs. "Hell, yeah! Never rode with no desperado before."

"You been riding with me for months, meathead. And besides, like I said, I ain't like that no more." Grinning, Kitt clapped the bigger man on the shoulder. "But thanks."

"Oh, and Miss Lucas?" he said, turning from the door as he put his hat back on. "That was mighty fine coffee. Thank you kindly."

Eleanor's hands were on her hips. "You only butter me up when you're after something, Dale."

"Uh, yeah...well, I was just wondering: do you think we could maybe borrow a couple of your departed mama's best table knives, in case things get hairy out there?"

"That's a dollar fifty gone up in smoke every time you pull the trigger, Sam. Just you keep that in mind."

Kitt hefted his bulging pocketful of shotgun shells, each one packed with gleaming silver buckshot. Silver bullets had been out of the question; there hadn't been time to cast and load proper rifle cartridges, and old black-powder guns firing silver balls were—with one exception—too slow and clumsy for the lunatic brawl they were expecting. Besides, everyone knows a scatter-gun's the only tool when you're serious about the job of killing something.

"A hell of a lot of whiskey we're shootin'," he muttered, staring down sadly at his sawed-off weapon. An ounce and a quarter of pure, deadly money crouched in that chamber, waiting to spring. The cold light of overcast early morning washed gray over everything.

"Keep your voice down, Dale," Sam whispered back, barely audible over the whistling wind. "And count your-self lucky you're buying your fool life so cheap." The pair were laying low in the tall grass, not a hundred yards from the big house of the Tumbling 'T'. They'd taken a couple of hours to crawl this far, getting into their position on this low hill, moving upwind so the wolf-men couldn't smell or hear them.

Sam looked out through the screen of grass, watching for movement near the house. The muddy yard was a churned-up mess around the smoking remains of what must have been one hell of a fire, a circle of charred wood at least five feet across. Somewhere off to his left, he knew, Quinney was taking up his own position. To Sam's right, invisible in a clump of trees and brush, Frank Grill was getting ready to make the shot that would tell them all whether Kitt was spending his fortune wisely.

They'd decided they needed a test before charging in there with guns blazing, just to make sure Doc's silver solution wasn't as mythical as they'd once thought were-wolves to be. So Frank had cast himself a few silver balls and hauled out his old black-powder gun. He'd been a fine sharpshooter back in the day—as fine as you could be with a musket—and if his target went down, that was the signal to move in. If the man-thing felt the same about silver as it felt about lead, well...they were all dead men anyway, weren't they?

Now it was just a matter of waiting for one of Neuman's wolves to make an appearance. The yard was currently deserted; the night-loving creatures were probably sleeping, just as Quinney guessed. Sam watched the muddy flat, trying hard to keep his eyes off the grisly bone pile heaped near the fire ring. It was an ugly jumble of remains—horse, human and otherwise—that would have turned his stomach even if the wind hadn't carried its stench to him. All that was left of a lot of good men had been tossed onto that pile, maybe his brother among them. Sam forced himself to look at something else, anything else.

There was movement in the doorway of the ranch house. One of the sheriff's goons, the thug they called Mule, was stepping out into the yard, squinting and scratching his behind. He looked like a normal man this morning—ugly as hell, but normal. Sam held his breath as he waited for Frank to take his shot.

A second flash of motion at the door of the house. A second man, one Sam couldn't immediately recognize, emerged to join Mule in the yard. Two sentries! This wasn't good. If Frank took one of them down, his position would be given away to the other, and there's no way he could reload that old gun of his in time to take a second shot. He had a shotgun with him too, but those things were *fast*. The big cowboy might not even have time to bring up the other gun before the wolf was on him.

Don't do it, Frank! Wait 'til we get one alone!

CRACK! The thunderclap of the black-powder gun broke the morning apart. The result of Frank's shot was spectacular. Mule staggered backward, doubling over; the ball had caught him square in the belly. Immediately, huge gouts of brilliant green flame began spewing from the hole in his guts. Screaming like a wounded animal, he fell back, clutching vainly at his burning stomach, and as he fell his body writhed with wild transformations, a chaos of fur and flesh, man-parts and wolf-parts shifting into and out of each other. Finally, the screaming stopped, the unholy green fires died and the monstrosity lay still in the mud.

But Mule's counterpart was anything but still. Momentarily stunned by his friend's shooting, he had quickly recovered, shifting in an eyeblink from nondescript human to seven-foot-tall wolf-thing. It wasn't hard to tell where that shot had come from—the dark cloud of gun-smoke drifted lazily south on the wind. The savage sentry launched himself toward Frank's stand of trees, a snarling nightmare moving on predator's legs.

"Frank!" Kitt was up and running, sprinting desperately to intercept the creature.

"Dale, no! We've got to..." But there was no stopping him. "Ah, hell," Sam muttered, standing and running after the other man. "I guess we *are* all in this together."

Another booming report rang out. Frank, still hidden by his little thicket, had managed to get a shot off. Sam saw the leaping monster spin in midair, howling in pain as green flames burst from its body. It landed on its feet though, clutching at a shoulder that spewed fireworks—Frank had only winged the thing. With a snarl of rage, it leaped into the trees. Even from a few dozen yards away, Sam heard the sickening, wet crunch that followed.

Kitt had run close enough for his sawed-off to be effective, and stopped to give a sharp whistle. The thing emerged from the trees, crouched low and growling. Inky fumes poured from its wounded shoulder, the left arm dangling uselessly, shivering between human and wolf shape. Its other claw was bright red with fresh blood. Yellow eyes glared with hate.

"Eat silver, you hairy freak." Kitt's shotgun barked, and a fountain of emerald flame appeared where the werewolf's head had been.

"Yeah, that was worth a buck and a half." Kitt popped another shell into his smoking gun.

By this time, there were another eight or so of the things on the way from the ranch house, howling their way across the muddy yard and up the rise to where the two men stood. Sam thought of Quinney, who still hadn't made himself seen. *That's it kid...stick to the plan. You're our ace in the hole if this goes even more wrong.*

"Dale, keep your head," Sam said quietly as they watched the pack of wolf-men snarling their way toward them. He raised up his double-barreled scattergun. "One man shoots while the other reloads. If we're both caught with empty guns, we're breakfast."

"Right. Good luck, Sam. It's been nice knowin' you."

For a while, it looked like they might make it. Once the pack of wolf-men learned respect for the cowboys' charmed ammunition, a lesson that cost them two more of their number, they kept their distance, circling the men who stood back-to-back, looking for openings. A few more of the things—those that were dumber, or braver, or more savage—went down after making wild solo rushes. The air was clotted with the stench of the weird fires that burned away their unnatural lives.

But their luck couldn't hold; there were just too many of the monsters, and the ones remaining got smart. Screaming in rage, a pair of the things leaped at Kitt from two sides while Sam was frantically reloading. One burst into flame before it hit the ground, its chest full of burning silver, but the other closed the distance and swung a huge clawed paw to gut the now-defenseless man with an underhand slash.

Fast as the thing was, the dark-haired bandit was quicker. As the beast's wicked talons flashed toward him, Kitt manage to swing his empty gun around and, grabbing the still-hot barrel, block the killing strike. Gun and man went flying from the force of the blow, and Kitt's back and head slammed into a tree with a sharp crack. When he dropped to the ground, he didn't get up.

"Dale!" Sam wrenched the breech of his loaded gun closed and snapped the weapon up, firing point-blank at the wolf-man. The thing flew backward, spinning, spewing electric flame. His feeling of satisfaction was brief. His heart went cold as he realized what he'd just done.

In his panic, he'd given the monster both barrels. His gun was empty.

A long growl like a laugh came from his left. Sam turned to face a huge wolf-man, fully eight feet tall if he was an inch, stalking slowly toward him. Teeth like knives were brilliant against the thing's shaggy midnight fur. A long, pink tongue licked black lips. A bright tin star hung against the creature's massive chest, dangling by a leather thong.

"Howdy, sheriff." Sam knew he was going to die. He thought of Eleanor.

"Sam!" It was Quinney, shouting from behind him. He'd crawled up through the grass from his position on the other end of the yard. "I...I can't take a shot without hitting you too!"

"Don't worry about me, kid," Sam said without shouting, not taking his eyes off the dark man-beast approaching him. Behind the huge werewolf, the remainder of the pack howled and jeered. "Save yourself. Run and gun, and you just might make it."

"Sam, I..."

"Go, damnit! We're done for." He could smell the matted fur of the animal that was once the sheriff. He could almost feel its breath. He knew this corrupted thing was going to take its time about killing him, and he wished he had a six-gun to deny it the pleasure. He closed his eyes.

There was a whistling sound in the air, followed by a meaty impact. Sam opened his eyes to find the black werewolf's chest had suddenly sprouted two feet of feathered wood. The thing looked stupidly down at the arrow sticking out of its body, reaching to pull it out.

It never got the chance. As Sam watched, horrified, the monster's flesh began to bubble and split in a pattern radiating out from the wound. The thing stumbled back, shreiking in pain as the blight spread across its huge body and strips of disintegrating flesh fell away, exposing ribs and bone. It was like watching a carcass rot in seconds rather than weeks. In the time it takes to draw one breath, there was nothing left of the sheriff but a bleached-white skeleton, a tin star dangling in its empty ribcage.

More arrows were whistling in. After an instant of screaming death that Sam would never forget no matter how hard he tried, there were only living men and dry bones in the grass. Sam whirled in the direction the arrows had come, and there on the ridge stood a trio of Indian braves and one unmistakable figure.

"Well I'll be...Dwayne Buckle!" The men were hurrying down the rise, and Sam started to run to meet them before rembering Dale Kitt, lying under the tree. He went to the fallen man's side just as he was regaining his senses.

"Uhhh...Sam? What...what happened? Did we..."

"Yeah, we did it, partner. We got 'em, no thanks to my own fool self. Here comes the man you want to thank for saving our skins." Buckle and the three braves were striding up through the grass.

"Hello, Sam. Sorry to cut it so close." The half-breed's voice was surprisingly deep, even for his broad six-six frame.

"Buckle, I ain't gonna complain." The blond foreman clasped the tall man's shoulder, shaking his hand. "I owe you my life. You gentlemen too...thank you all." His composure was shot; shaking with adrenaline, he slumped against the tree that had blocked Kitt's flight.

The wiry little man was still sitting on the ground, amazed to be alive. "I just don't believe it. I owe you big,

Dwayne. And, yeah, you fellas too. I don't know what you did, but thanks for doing it."

Quinney had come running up, excited. "Hey, Dwayne! Let me guess. Aconite, right?"

"Yeah, that's what you folks call it, all right."

"But how did you know about it? I mean, how did you know it would work on...on these things?"

"I didn't, but our medicine man did. We've got our own wolf-men, you know? I just bet that local medicine works on foreigners too."

Sam was gathering his wits about him. "I guess we can all pat each other on the back when this is all over. We've still got a piece of work ahead of us." He nodded toward the ranch house. "Unless Neuman's hightailed it out the back way."

Dwayne shook his head, glossy black braids dancing on his shoulders. "No way. We've got the place surrounded. If he ran, he's dead already."

"Well." Sam stood up, breaking open his shotgun and filling it with another three dollars' worth of Kitt's loot. "What do you say we go pay him a visit, huh?"

They walked up to the house in a single line, weapons at the ready, through the sticking mud of the yard, past the hideously piled evidence of the werewolves' crimes. The once-grand house was dilapidated, paint peeling and shingles flaking off, the steps and porch missing boards—a house for animals, not men. Sam stepped forward and faced the weatherbeaten front doors, their windows opaqued by layers of grime. A light drizzle had begun to fall.

"Neuman!" Sam shouted. "Neuman, come on out! It's over!"

Even muffled by the doors, there was no mistaking the note of hysterical madness that tinged the precise European voice that replied; Neuman had gone right round the bend.

"Over? *Over?* It'll never be over, human! You know it, and all your ancestors knew it: this world, this *universe,* is filled with beings that hate you. The day will come when all your cities and lights and little toy guns won't save you. The age of man will end!"

The high-pitched laugh coming from inside the house gave cold goosepimples to the men in the yard; it was a barking cackle, the sound of a mad dog.

"Well, I guess I don't know about any of that, Neuman," Sam called back. "But I'm pretty sure it's over for you."

"Ha! Even there you're wrong, McKenna, even there. I have what you might call an ace up my sleeve. I still win, McKenna! I still win!"

There was a sound of something scrambling on wood just behind the doors, the clinking of metal on metal. Sam brought his shotgun up tight to his shoulder, just as the doors burst open.

If he'd thought the thing that used to be the sheriff had been big, the red-furred monster that came snarling out of the ranch house made that black beast look like a lap-dog. Hunched, its head barely cleared the big doorframe; it almost filled the width of the doorway. Its broad head was all razor teeth and wild eyes, and from its neck and wrists dangled heavy iron chains. But worse than any of that, worse than all that put together, was the tattered remnant of an exquisitely embroidered buckskin jacket that still hung around its shaggy shoulders.

"Sweet Jesus," Kitt whispered, a million miles behind Sam.

Sam's gun wavered. "Oh...oh, no. No, Davey...he can't have..." The hulking thing on the porch didn't wait for Sam to finish his sentence. With an animal roar, it leaped forward, making straight for the stunned foreman.

Sam looked into the thing's yellow eyes, two fireballs above the tearing, ripping white of its mouth. In the instant between the porch and his own throat, Sam searched desperately for anything human there, anything of his brother. He didn't find it.

Two barrels of pure silver exploded into a blossom of unholy green flame.

The Boto

When we think of dolphins, the creatures that most commonly come to mind are bottlenose dolphins of the "Flipper" type, playful and intelligent creatures of the sea. But numerous dolphin species are also to be found in rivers around the world, from China's Yellow River to India's sacred Ganges. Of these freshwater dolphins one of the strangest is the Amazon river dolphin, named by science as Inia geoffrensis and sometimes referred to as the "pink" dolphin—but more commonly known as the boto.

The boto is the largest of the river dolphins, with adult males weighing in at up to 400 pounds. A slow-moving creature, especially when compared with its speedy cousins in the sea, the boto makes up for its sluggish pace with an amazing degree of flexibility. Unlike most other dolphins, the bones in the boto's neck aren't fused together, enabling it to turn its head in any direction. This comes in handy when its river habitat undergoes its regular cycle of flooding: the exceptionally maneuverable boto has no problem dodging between the submerged trunks of trees in search of a tasty meal of fish.

It is a common misconception, perhaps given credibility by the creature's small eyes and the murky waters in which it swims, that the boto is blind. In fact, the boto's vision is quite sharp. Even sharper, though, is its sense of echolocation, the ability to "see" underwater by listening to the echoes of their high-pitched clicks as they bounce off objects and other animals. Again, this adaptation allows it to easily navigate the clutter of flooded areas.

Like the more familiar dolphins, the boto *is highly intelligent, as well as naturally curious and playful. It's perhaps inevitable that an animal so strange, and yet so strangely humanlike, would claim a prominent place in the folklore and culture of the people who come into contact with it. As millennia of sailors and fishermen have done with the* boto*'s sea-swimming relatives, so have the people of the river spun webs of folklore, legend and superstition around their mysterious dolphins.*

Central to these beliefs is the encantado, *water spirits that are able to take both human and* boto *form. Like the* boto, *they are mischievous and curious. They are very interested in humans, and love to take human form and move around in dryland society. They are very fond music and dancing, often coming out of the water to attend parties and festivals.*

But the encantado, *like all nature spirits, are wild, unpredictable, and dangerous; their mischief can become malice, their curiosity can become lust. This is when the* encantado *expresses the darker side of the* boto*'s nature, and becomes a deadly predator. Taking the form of a handsome man, usually wearing an impeccable white suit in an old-fashioned cut, the* encantado *will join a human festival in order to seduce a young woman—whom he may have already spotted and fixed on while in dolphin form. His charm is hypnotic, perhaps even telepathic, and unless the proper intervention is taken, or the woman's will can overcome his powers, he will lure her to the river and take her down with him to his home in the underwater city of spirits known as the* Encante. *Rarely are these unfortunate girls seen again on dry land.*

The story you are about to read concerns a young American woman—urbane, educated, skeptical and more than a little jaded—and her brush with one of these mysterious shapeshifting creatures. As with all true contacts with the worlds of magic, her encounter will leave her profoundly changed.

The boat chugged upstream, the green of the river rolling past to the beat of the ancient engine. The wild wall of rain forest rose from the flooded banks of the wide river, over living water that had come from the Andes 3000 miles away, and wouldn't join the sea until another 1000 had passed. This was the Amazon, the greatest river in the world, lifeblood of the Earth, source of legends and place of magic.

Christine Moura was bored by it.

She'd seen rivers before; half her career had been spent on rivers. The sacred Ganges, the rugged Colorado, the wild Mackenzie, the "blue" Danube—she'd photographed them all. Another village, another adorable group of children, another "striking image"—pretty pictures to pay the bills.

When did I get so cynical, she thought, pushing a curl of black hair out of her eyes and trying to notice the magic in the slow procession of forest and muddy water. Years had passed since she'd felt the thrill of discovery and adventure at her job. Her *job*. Not her passion, not her vocation; her job. Even accepting this assignment, flying down to Brazil to do a feature on the *boto*, the weird freshwater dolphins that inhabit the twists and turns of the Amazon, was more robotic response than conscious decision. Any successful New York freelancer has the built-in reflex of never refusing easy work.

Christine sighed and sipped jet-black coffee from the heavy ceramic cup cradled in her hands. It was hot, and strong enough to be called powerful—good working-man's coffee. She was taking another sip, savoring its warmth despite the oppressive heat of the June day, when a heavily accented voice called out cheerfully from behind her.

"Hello, Miss Moura! How do you like my coffee?"

The photographer turned to see Diogo, the boat's captain and her guide, coming around from the cabin where his ship's mate and brother-in-law Aldemar manned the wheel. The weatherbeaten boatman was smiling, as usual, and wearing one of the Hawaiian shirts he was so fond of. He'd been recommended to her by Dr. Tyndall, the English zoologist she'd hoped to interview but who'd been unexpectedly called away. So far Diogo had been an excellent substitute—friendly, proud to share his knowledge of the river and its secrets, and quite photogenic.

"*Sim, e' muito bom,*" she replied in the simple but adequate Portuguese she'd learned from her grandparents. "It is very good."

"Yes, yes!" Diogo exclaimed, grinning even more broadly. "I make it very strong, the best way." He sat down with a sigh on a large coil of rope opposite the one Christine was perched on, and they sat watching the river in silence. Out of the corner of her eye, she could see him glancing at her curiously before he spoke again.

"Miss Moura," he asked, smiling but with an unreadable look in his eye, "you do not have any babies, do you?"

"Um...no, no, I don't," she replied, a little surprised at the directness of the question.

Diogo grinned again and slapped his knee. "Ah! I knew it! I can always tell."

"Oh?" Christine asked, amused despite the personal nature of the conversation. "And how can you tell?"

"Because, the women with no babies," Diogo responded with mock seriousness, "they hug their coffee instead."

Christine looked down at her hands wrapped around the big mug, rolled her eyes and grinned along with her guide. Setting down the cup, she swung up her camera and began snapping photos of the laughing boatman.

"Ah, don't take any more pictures of me," he protested, though he clearly enjoyed the attention, striking rugged poses straight out of some jungle adventure movie. "Save your film for the *boto* when we see them."

"And when will that be?" she asked, her camera's shutter and motor drive still clicking and whirring. "Seems like we've come a long way up the river."

"Very soon now, very soon," he replied. "There is a place up ahead, a big curve in the river the dolphins like very much. Shallow water, lots to eat." He sat back down on his pile of rope and faced her directly, leaning forward with hands clasped and elbows on his knees.

"Now I have to tell you," he continued in a serious tone. "You must be very careful with the *boto*. They are friendly, yes, but some of them are maybe not what they seem."

"Not what they—oh! You mean how some are supposed to be able to change shape and walk around on land as people?" She'd come across this piece of folklore while researching the dolphins, and she found the idea of a "were-dolphin" to be more humorous than anything else. She wasn't surprised to hear Diogo speaking of it—folktales die hard—but she was amused to see him taking it so very seriously.

"No!" the Brazilian barked, with a slash of his hand. "Not dolphins, and not people. They are the *encantados*, the Enchanted Ones. Powerful spirits that take either shape when they like. They live in the city of spirits under the river, a place called the *Encante*. The *encantado* men, they like human girls very much, and they love human music. So they come up out of the river when there is a *festa*, a celebration. They join the party, then put a spell on their chosen girl, lead her down to the river and..."

Diogo stopped himself, looking embarrassed. He coughed and continued in a lighter tone. "There is a big *festa* tomorrow, the Feast of Saint John. It is the big day of what we call *Festa Junina*, the June Feast. You are going to take pictures of the *festa*." It wasn't a question, but Christine nodded yes.

"Good, good! It is a very fun party. Just be careful, watch out for mysterious men who want to get you alone."

He gave her a stern look, and Christine couldn't help but give a little laugh; telling a born-and-raised New York girl to beware of strange men was like telling a boat captain to keep an eye out for rocks. Still, seeing Diogo's earnestness, she decided to play along. Besides, she wanted to know more about these superstitions; they'd be great "local color" when she wrote her piece.

"OK then—no strange men for me. But tell me, how can I tell a normal man from an *encantado*? I don't want to have to avoid every man in town just because one of them might want to drag me to the river."

"It is very simple, Miss Moura," replied Diogo in a matter-of-fact tone. "Just ask him to take off his hat. The *encantado* can't transform completely into a man, so there is always a bald spot on top of his head where the dolphin's blowhole is. If a man won't take off his hat, then you should worry."

Christine smiled. "That easy, huh? Thanks for the tip, Diogo." She turned and looked down into the murky Amazon, feeling the bass vibrations of the old boat in her body and trying to visualize a magical city under all that green water. "Diogo," she asked after a while, not looking up from the river, "do you really believe in the *encantados*, in their underwater city?" When he didn't answer immediately, she turned back from the side of the boat to see him gazing up at the sky in thought.

"Well..." he answered in a slow drawl, choosing his words carefully, "my *avô*, my grandfather, used to tell me stories of the Enchanted Ones, how when he was a boy there were many around trying to live as people in the villages. Not long ago, you could still find *encantado* written on birth certificates when a baby's father was unknown.

"My grandmother on my mother's side," Diogo continued. "She is a *bruxa*, a wise woman. She believes, but says there are too many people now, too much noise and stink of gasoline in the cities and towns for the *encantados* to stand. She says they almost always stay in the *Encante* now."

"But what about *you*, Diogo?" Christine pressed. "What do *you* think? Do you believe that the *boto* come out of the river and walk on land?"

"Oh, yes," Diogo answered brightly, laughing at Christine's look of surprise. "*That* I believe. I have seen it with my own eyes!"

The boatman laughed again, harder, at the journalist's slack-jawed speechlessness. "But, it's not like you think," he continued.

"Not like I think? What do you mean?" Christine was confused, thinking she'd missed something.

"I mean I've seen dolphins, real dolphins, walking on the ground," Diogo answered, still chuckling. "When the river floods like it is now, the *boto* swim out into the floodplains. That's why their sonar is even better than dolphins in the sea. They need to find their way around trees and logs in very muddy water. But the river, it can go back down very quickly and sometimes leave the *boto* behind. Then they must drag and roll themselves back to the deep water. I have seen it twice before."

Christine nodded and smiled; this was great stuff for her article. "Do you think that's how the stories of the *encantados* began?" she asked. "The legends of dolphins turning into humans and coming up onto land?"

Diogo looked at her for a moment before making an elaborate shrug. "Maybe, maybe," he answered without conviction, turning to watch the approaching bend in the river. "The stories are very old. Who knows where they come from?" Turning back to the boat's enclosed cockpit, he shouted to his mate in Portuguese, "Hey, Aldemar! Slow it right down!"

The engine's throaty growl subsided quickly to a low purr, and it felt like a deafening silence had fallen over the boat. As the ringing in her ears subsided, the sounds of the rainforest came to Christine—bird calls, the cries of unknown animals, the rustle and sigh of the trees themselves. In this new quiet, the magic of the Amazon seemed much nearer than it had when the antiquated diesel engine had been lugging the boat through the water. There was expectation in the air; Christine checked her gear and readied her camera.

"There," said Diogo softly, pointing ahead and to the side. "Look. The *boto* comes."

A pink shape approached slowly through the water, propelled by long muscular fins like wings, breaking the surface a few dozen feet from Diogo's idling tub. It was like no dolphin she had ever seen, vastly different from the "Flipper" variety. A sturdy but sleek body ended in a large head and a very long curved beak. Small eyes above bulging cheeks peered intently at her across the water, sending a self-conscious shiver down her spine; there was so much intelligence, even humor, in that look. She was transfixed, frozen in space and time as this strange creature of the river seemed to take her measure. Pure photographer's reflex brought the camera up for a shot.

With the snap of the shutter and the whirr of the camera's motorized winder, the river dolphin flicked its body and plunged once more under the surface of the Amazon. Christine was afraid she'd somehow frightened it away, and turned worriedly back to Diogo.

"It...did I...?" she began, stopping short when she saw the boatman's smile.

"No, Miss Moura; he'll be back. That one was just scouting...look!"

She followed his pointing hand to see a crowd of dolphin shapes, some pink, some blue-gray, some nearly white, approaching the boat. There were at least a dozen she could see, and it seemed like more were coming. Her dependable old Nikon whirred and clicked, capturing the scene as the *boto* welcoming committee approached. Their humped, finless backs broke the surface on both sides of the boat as the curious creatures circled. There were at least twenty now that she could see, and the sight of them filled her with a joy she hadn't felt in years.

"They're beautiful! And there's so many!" she cried, her camera never stopping. "Is this...is this normal? I thought they didn't form such large groups."

"No, no they don't," Diogo replied, with an uneasy note in his voice that made Christine look up from her camera. "No, this is very...strange." Seeing her confused look, he quickly brightened his tone. "But very good for pictures, yes? Maybe they like you!" There was something in his forced smile that disturbed her, but she soon forgot about it when she turned her eyes and camera back to the *boto* spiraling around the boat.

It *did* seem like they liked her, and they *were* very good for pictures; it was almost as if they were posing for her, giving her the perfect shots she wanted. They leaped and played for action shots, and when she wanted close-ups, the first bright-pink dolphin she'd seen reappeared at the side of the boat, grinning like a catalog model inches away from her camera. She'd come get the underwater shots her editors wanted when she finally hooked up with Dr.

Tyndall, but these would almost be enough. Leaping dolphins, lazing dolphins, mothers with calves, one roll of film, two rolls, three—she was enchanted. For the first time in a long time, Christine was having fun taking pictures. She was reaching for another roll of film when she heard Diogo clear his throat.

"Miss Moura," he said, looking nervously at the *boto*, "we must be going now. It is not good to disturb the *boto* for so long."

"So *long*?" she protested. "But we only just got here!"

"It is enough, Miss Moura. We should not be troubling the dolphins like this, and it will be getting dark soon." Red-faced, he shot another glance at the group of graceful animals. Christine's pink friend floated and watched them intently. "Please, we must leave now. Aldemar! Go!"

The engine roared to life instantly, as if the pilot had been waiting with his hand on the throttle for the captain's signal. The *boto* scattered as the old boat began to turn around, heading downstream. Christine pulled at the flustered boatman's sleeve.

"Diogo, what's going on," she demanded. "You're being paid good money to take..."

"To take you to take pictures of the *boto*, yes. And you took many pictures. Now we must go back. There are...government regulations. A big group like that, we should not disturb them."

There was an air of finality in the Brazilian's voice. He was right, though; she *did* get a lot of good pictures. She walked to the back of the boat and watched the riverbend recede, feeling Diogo's eyes on her back as she leaned against the rail. The pink dolphin was still floating there, watching her, and she again felt the electric thrill of connection.

It *was* getting dark, and Christine felt a tiredness come over her. When her dolphin had disappeared from view, she lay back on a tangle of netting and closed her eyes. The heat, the journey, the stories, the excitement of the shoot, the remarkable dolphins—it had been a long day.

Sleep took her quickly, and she slept all the way back to Manaus. Her dreams were filled with the forest, with the river, with cool flowing water around the architecture of an underwater city, with the sleek and smiling faces of the *boto*.

The *festa* was, as Diogo had promised, a good party. More natural and folksy than Rio's outrageous *Carneval*, and nothing at all like the boozy Mardi Gras in New Orleans. It was a beautiful swirling chaos of noise and light and color, and Christine moved through it in a joyful daze. Diogo had protested when she'd decided to wander out on her own, but he'd finally relented, looking miserable and begging her again to be careful. The shouts of vendors mixed with the sound of laughter and the music of folksingers and Brazilian pop songs as she walked. Bright flashes of colorful costumes caught the light of lanterns and fireworks. Habit, and the hope of maybe capturing even a fraction of this experience on film, kept her snapping pictures.

It had been with her all day, this giddy sensation of delight. Manaus, the city she'd first seen as just another faded colonial town, had transformed itself overnight for her. Everything was more interesting, beautiful, captivating.

Earlier that day she'd visited the opera house, the *Teatro Amazonas*, pride of the city. While reading the guidebooks on the flight from New York, she'd dismissed the elaborate theater as a backwater pipe-dream, a vulgar attempt by slave-driving plantation owners to buy a bit of Continental credibility for their isolated outpost. But then she stood in the hall and looked up at the ceiling. It had been designed to look like the view from underneath the Eiffel Tower, and she saw more than the gaudy tastes of the cruel rubber barons. She saw a dream of beauty and elegance, of high European culture in the deepest heart of the New World, of a glittering new empire on the banks of the Amazon. It had nearly brought her to tears.

Now, in the happily boiling crowd of the *festa*, she was captivated by another, older, European import as she watched a group of brightly costumed young people dance the *quadrilha*, a theatrical square dance introduced by French missionaries and adapted over generations into a uniquely Brazilian affair. The dancers swirled in their formations to the wailing harmonies of the accordion, spinning in squares, circles and stars as the caller dictated. Jokes and answering laughter came from the dancers and the crowd as the pattern moved and shifted in perfect clockwork arrangement. Partners passed back and forth, twirling, embracing and releasing, hypnotic.

"It's wonderful to watch, isn't it?"

With the question came a light touch on her shoulder, and Christine turned to face the most handsome man she had ever seen. He wore an immaculate white linen suit, and his glossy black hair tumbled from beneath an old-fashioned straw hat. It framed a young face with Indian features, made all the more striking by the strangely pale tone of his smooth skin, lighter than any Indian she'd met. But it was the eyes that caught and held her. Not large, but deep as dark water. Those laughing eyes were for an instant the only thing in her world, seeming to reflect the whirling patterns of the *quadrilha*.

"I...y-es, it is," she stammered, tearing herself away from his bottomless gaze and turning back to the dancers, her knees suddenly weak. The dance came to its perfectly choreographed close and the onlookers called for another. Christine could feel the man's presence near her as the caller jokingly made a big production out of giving the crowd what it wanted.

"All right, all right," the big, laughing man called out, accepting and quickly downing a drink offered by a nearby companion. "But some of these fine dancers have been at it for hours—the *quadrilha* needs fresh legs! Who will come and join us here?"

An electric chill ran over Christine's skin, goosebumps of mixed dread and anticipation. *Oh, no*, she thought. *Not me.*

"Miss, would you like to try the *quadrilha*?" That voice at her shoulder again, soft and warm but strangely high-pitched. Christine willed herself not to make eye contact as she answered.

"No, no, I, uh...I can't. I don't...I don't know how to dance." The response sounded weak even to herself, until she realized with a shock she'd responded in Portuguese.

"Ah! You speak Portuguese! Then you have nothing to worry about; just follow the caller's instructions and mind the other dancers. The *quadrilha* has patterns, and the

right way to move is the only one that doesn't feel wrong."
She could feel the smile in his voice.

"No, really. Thank you, but I—I shouldn't," she replied,
her gaze focused on the ground.

The man stepped around to face her. She noticed his
perfectly polished shoes as a wide but elegant hand
invited her to dance. Her eyes couldn't help but move up
from that hand, up the white arm of the outdated but
beautifully tailored suit, to the lean, pale face and the
spinning whirlpool of those eyes.

"Miss, I promise...I would not let you embarrass yourself." His playful grin showed brilliant rows of small, even
teeth, and Christine felt her reluctance leave her like a
weight being lifted off her body. She rested her hand in
his, felt the soft coolness of his skin and allowed herself to
be led into the dance.

The caller shouted out, the accordion cried and the
quadrilha began. Slow at first, with bows and curtseys,
and easy laps around the perimeter of the dance. Bold
advances and flirtatious retreats followed, all called out
in a strange mix of Portuguese and the original French.
The patterns moved and shifted, and Christine moved
and shifted with them, stepping and double-stepping,
carried along almost effortlessly by the logic of the pattern and the gentle guidance of her partner. Even when
the tides of the *quadrilha* drew them apart, she could feel
his presence watching her, supporting her. The only hin-
drance was her camera, which banged at her hip as she
spun through the steps. The *quadrilha*, for all its formal-
ity, is not a solemn dance, and her trusty Nikon did not
go unnoticed.

"Hey, colonel!" shouted one man as he stepped back from his lady as one figure ended. "Keep it simple, eh? There's a tourist here!"

The quick-tongued caller rode the wave of laughter as he replied. "*You* keep it simple, left-feet! The tourist seems to be doing just fine. Accordion, rip it up! Everybody, form the Star!"

The caller was right; she *was* doing just fine. Her self-consciousness and doubt faded as the dancers around her formed the geometric *estrela*, the Star. Out on one of radiating points, Christine kept the pace as the formation whirled. She was spinning in infinity, lost in the form and flow of the *quadrilha*, a molecule in a chemical reaction, connected to every other dancer—connected most of all to the lean, graceful figure opposite her, who sent cool electricity through her body when they touched, and who warmed her with a wink when they did not. The endless dance proceeded to its conclusion. She was in love.

The accordion sighed out its last note, the dancers made their last bows and the boisterous crowd cheered out their approval.

"That was wonderful, miss; thank you for the dance. You are a natural!" The beautiful man in white linen threw his arms around her in a spontaneously joyful embrace that took her breath away. He lifted her ever so slightly from the ground and spun her through a half-turn. The press of festival-goers around them began to disperse and thin out, as the caller and the accordion player—and the remaining dancers—seemed to be determined, this time, to take a refreshment break.

"Thank *you*..." she began, stepping back with a smile and a questioning look.

"Oh! Please forgive me for not introducing myself." He made a little bow that would have looked contrived or theatrical from anyone else. Tipping his wide-brimmed straw hat, he showed a full head of luxurious dark hair. Christine laughed inwardly, remembering Diogo's earnest warning against men who refused to uncover their heads.

"My name is Benigno," he said. "And you are?"

She smiled at the name—*Benigno*, from the Latin for "good" or "kind." Like everything about him, from his suit to his smile, it fit perfectly. She answered his bow with a playful imitation of a formal curtsey. "Christine," she smiled. "It's a pleasure to meet you, Benigno. Thank you very much for the dancing lesson."

They'd been speaking in Portuguese, but Benigno switched over to perfect English with an accent just thick enough to be exotic. "Please, Christine, call me Ben. It's what all my other friends from New York call me. And it was hardly a lesson. You are a natural."

Christine blushed again. "Well, again, thank you, Ben." Her heart was beating fast, her mind swimming with the sights and sounds of the *festa* and the limitless eyes of the man who stood smiling at her. She felt as though she were about to leap from a seaside cliff, fear and excitement mingling in an ecstasy of anticipation.

"Would you...would you like to take a walk with me?" she asked, hoping he wouldn't notice the tremble in her voice.

"Christine, I'd be delighted to," he said, offering his arm with a courtly flourish. She slipped one hand around to rest inside his elbow and with the other lightly held his upper arm. Close together, nestled like lovers, they set off happily through the streets of Manaus.

"So, you've been to New York?" she asked after they'd walked for a while in silence, simply watching and enjoying the tropical festivities that bubbled around them like scenes in a dream.

"Oh, yes," he answered in a voice that might have been shrill if it hadn't also been so gentle. "I studied literature at Columbia on exchange for a year, and I've been back once since. It is a costly trip," he added, with a faraway look in his eyes, "but I just love visiting your world."

Christine laughed. " 'My world?' It may seem like it at times, but New York is hardly an alien planet."

It was Ben's turn to look flustered; spots of color rose on his pale cheeks. "Sorry. That's the wrong word, isn't it? I meant your *country*. But it is like another world, isn't it? So new, so fast, with everything the whole planet has to offer at your fingertips. Not like this place. Here, nothing ever *really* changes. It simply keeps moving just fast enough so the forest and the river can't close in and swallow it all." He gave a little sigh. "I've seen enough of Manaus to last me 200 years."

Christine sensed Benigno had more to say on the subject, but she didn't press him on it. There would be time enough to dive into his depths—an entire lifetime together to learn each other's secrets, if she got her heart's desire. Instead, she continued brightly: "Well, I suppose I thought so too, when I first saw the place. But...something's changed. I find it remarkably charming." She smiled up at him.

He gave back a grin of perfect white teeth. "Ah!" he exclaimed grandly, like a stage magician. "That's the magic of the *festa*, you see? Like any city wrapped in a festival, when Manaus fills with celebration, with the unbridled energy of hundreds of thousands of people, it becomes a different place, an enchanted place, a place of wonder and miracles. That's why I come here."

"Oh, you don't live in the city?" Christine asked, charmed his idealistic approach to the science of partying.

"No, my home is elsewhere," he answered, looking off into the distance as though he could see his hometown in the distance.

"Is it very far away?"

"Actually, it is quite nearby, but it's not easy to get to." His eyes had a faraway look again.

"Tell me about it," Christine said, almost in a whisper.

"It's...it's the most wonderful place in the world," he said, haltingly, as if searching for the right words. "Clean, wide streets and beautiful buildings, lit up always with lamps and lanterns of all colors, too many to count. Food, and music, and laughter all the time, no fighting except in sport. Hidden away, unspoiled..." His voice trailed off.

"It sounds like paradise, Benigno," Christine said, knowing how homesickness can make even the plainest little village seem like a Garden of Eden. "Why do you leave?"

He looked back to her, blinking, as if she had asked the most obvious of questions. "Because," he began, in a matter-of-fact tone, "there isn't a woman like you there."

They passed by a small plaza where a ceremonial pole had been decorated with flowers and ribbons. The pole was greased, and at the top were brightly colored bundles, small presents and cash money. A sizeable crowd had gathered to cheer on those who tried to shimmy up the slippery log for the prizes. The sharp, sweet smell of *cachaca*, the sugarcane liquor that is the national spirit of Brazil, filled the air as the noisy throng surged around the plaza. An over-refreshed partygoer lurched out of the chaos and staggered into Christine, splashing a bit of a warm, spicy-smelling drink on her blouse and slurring out an incomprehensible apology before weaving back into the mass of people.

From inside his jacket Ben pulled out a green silk cloth and dabbed at the little damp spot on Christine's shoulder.

"Thanks, Ben; it's not too bad. I guess you have to expect to be spilled on in a party like this. That's a beautiful handkerchief, by the way." The square of cloth he was using was a rich, shimmering blue-green with traces of exquisitely delicate embroidery around the edge.

"You like it? It belonged to my aunt. Please," he said, folding the cloth back into a neat square and offering it to her. "Take it. As something to remember me by."

"Ben, I couldn't! Are you sure?" He smiled and pressed it gently into her hand; the silk felt cool on her palm. She kept it in her hand as they resumed their stroll, talking and laughing about their travels, absorbing the magic of the night.

For a long time they walked, their path taking them along the river until they were far from the noise and the crowds of the *festa*. The streets were almost deserted, but, walking with Ben, Christine wasn't afraid of who or what might lurk in the alleys and shadows. She knew she was safe. The air seemed fragrant, the stillness sweetened with moonlight. Their conversation lapsed gently into contented silence by the time they came upon a low concrete wall and sat down to watch the river flow by.

"Don't you think it's lovely?" Ben asked quietly, after a long while had passed. Christine agreed that it was as lovely as anything she'd ever seen. The sound of lapping water soothed her and called to her as the silver moon joined the lights of the town in reflecting off the mirrored surface. The moving river broke everything up into an ever-shifting constellation of liquid jewels. And under that clear shining surface were black depths, endless expanses of cool, living water.

She turned to him. His eyes were like the river, dark reflecting pools that held her and drew her in. She moved closer to him, until her warm lips met with his soft and cool ones; they kissed gently, without lust or desperation. The whole world spun around her, orbiting the point where they touched, surrounding her in waves of joy as their souls poured into each other. It was perfect, impossibly perfect, and she was happily losing herself.

He broke the kiss, leaving her breathless, and again enveloped her with his bottomless eyes as her held her hands in his.

"Come with me into the river," he said. "The night is perfect for a swim."

"A swim?" she asked dreamily. "A swim. Yes, into the river. But..." She felt lost, dazed; she knew only that she needed to be with him.

"Please, Christine. Come with me. It will be perfect. Everything will be perfect. " He was standing now, pale in the moonlight, holding out his hands to her. His linen suit was gone except for the flowing white pants; his feet were bare. Trembling, unable to look away from those eyes, she stood and let her blouse and skirt fall away. Taking his hand, she followed him into the darkness of the river.

Black water—cool and pure, shining with pieces of the moon like diamonds—swallowed them as they embraced each other. His arms were strong around her as they moved deeper into the endless river, feet clear of the soft mud of the bottom. Her lips were on his as they fell deeper into each other, deeper into the watery darkness where a warm emerald glow waited for them.

No! This isn't right!

Something broke loose inside Christine, the bred-in-the-bone reflexes of a lifetime spent in New York subway stations and dark streets. They were under the water and he was dragging her down, drowning her, his arms like bars of padded iron. She struggled against him, yearning for the surface, unable to break his grip. She fought like a wild animal, biting, gouging, kneeing, pulling hair. Then she felt a thickly woven mat of perfect black hair come away from his smooth scalp.

Just when she thought she could fight no longer, the unbreakable grip was gone and she floated free. Consciousness slipped away from her, and the last thing she felt was a sleek, powerful shape speeding away from her, silhouetted against an brilliant vision of radiant green.

Beautiful buildings, wide streets...lamps and lanterns, too many to count...hidden away...unspoiled...

Christine woke slowly. She was in a white hospital room under cool, crisp bedsheets. Her hair spread its black tangle over the pillow as she licked her dry lips and let out a small sigh. A nurse, bustling nearby, hurried over and made the usual bedside checks.

"Good, you're awake," the plump, dark woman said in brisk Portuguese. "You just lie back and rest while I fetch the doctor." She was gone in a rustle of starched cloth before Christine could speak. Dazed and weak, Christine looked around the room, trying to focus her eyes, groping for clarity—the IV tube plugged and taped to her arm; the empty bed across the aisle, unmade as the nurse had left it; the weak gray light of the curtained window, beyond which rain was falling.

What happened to me?

Remembering was like sifting through a scattered pile of magazine clippings, a jumble of images, emotions and half-memories. She tried to put the pieces into some kind of order. There was the city, the *festa*, the noise and chaos, a beautiful young man in white. *Did that really happen?* The walking and talking, the riverside, the water and then...Nausea rose up to surround her in a grip of green. Overwhelmed, she sobbed in fear and frustration.

She heard the footsteps at the door. A doctor entered the room, and she felt an unmistakable change in the air. The physician, a tall, middle-aged man with steel-rimmed glasses on a blunt-featured face, swept up to her bedside. After a routine greeting and a quick glance at her chart, he began the examination.

"How do you feel, Miss Moura?" he asked, as one big thumb pried open her eyelid and his penlight shined in her eyes. "Follow the light, please."

"I...I feel weak. Nauseous. Thirsty. Cold. Confused."

"Hm. Well, you're still in shock, and before we got you on the IV you were dehydrated and your blood-sugar levels were critically low. Can you tell me what happened?"

"I don't know, doctor. It's hard to remember, everything seems like a blur. There was...I was at the festival, and I met a man, I think. We went walking, and...and I don't know what happened to me." Tears began gathering again in the corners of her eyes.

"OK, take it easy," he said, lacking the appropriate bedside manner. "You were found this morning by the river, soaking wet and...partially unclothed, half-conscious and delirious with shock. My examination revealed no evidence of sexual assault, and blood tests showed no drugs or toxins beyond a moderate alcohol level. You understand that the police want to speak with you?"

Christine nodded, feeling very frightened and vulnerable.

"All right, then. You just rest, and I'll check in with you later." He stood and walked out, but stopped at the door to turn back to her.

"Oh, there's one more thing you should know. I have you on a broad-spectrum antibiotic, just in case. That part of the river is like an open sewer. Please report any itching, rashes or respiratory problems to a nurse immediately." He strode out of the room, leaving the place feeling quiet and empty. Christine lay back, shivering and exhausted, and listened to the sound of rain on the window.

The police arrived shortly. The businesslike young officer was clearly not impressed with a young woman tourist who let herself be led off down a deserted street by some stranger. Numb, still not thinking clearly, she responded to his questions as well as she could in her scattered state. When it was clear he wasn't going to get much more than vague half-answers, he stood up, frowning.

"Miss, I don't know what's happened to you. Me, I'd say you were drunk, or drugged, but the doctor says no. If you *do* remember something, please call this number." He placed a card on the bedside table. "You know, there's not much chance we'll find this fellow."

"I know," Christine said.

"Well. Please watch yourself, and be careful in the future. There is somebody outside anxious to see you. I'll send him in."

The cop left, not shutting the door behind him, and Christine heard a murmur of conversation from out in the corridor. When the door opened again, a weathered man in a bright Hawaiian shirt entered, carrying a large plastic bag and escorting a scowling old woman.

"Diogo!" Christine exclaimed, smiling. A familiar face was just what she needed.

"Miss Moura, thank God you're all right!" The boatman's face was a mask of concern. "When you went off by yourself, I worried that you'd be..." He broke off, embarrassed. "Well, that something bad like this would happen to you. I went looking for you, down by the river, hoping...but when I saw you there, lying like you were dead, I couldn't believe it. I thought you were...lost."

"So, it was you who found me? Diogo, thank you, but...but that's amazing; what are the odds? How did you know where I was? Did you follow me?"

Diogo glanced nervously at the old woman. Her skin was like the husk of a walnut and her eyes were hawk's eyes. "I, ah...I had an idea where I might find you. I mean, there are certain places that...well, certain places where, ah, things like this are more likely to happen." He coughed uncomfortably and put a hand on the old woman's shoulder, as if to change the subject. "Miss Moura, I'd like you to meet my grandmother."

"Pleased to meet you," said Christine, even more confused. Diogo's grandmother, who he'd once said was some kind of medicine woman, didn't answer, but came up to the bed and began her own version of the doctor's examination, poking and prodding her, feeling her hair, smelling her breath, muttering and whispering all the while. When she'd finished, she turned to her grandson and nattered angrily in a dialect Christine couldn't follow.

In a tone halfway between soothing and pleading, Diogo answered back in the same manner. His grandmother replied with a dismissive wave and a curse that Christine *could* translate. Reaching into the battered patent-leather purse she carried slung over her shoulder, the old woman pulled out a fistful of something and turned back to the bed, flinging out her arm with a shout. A cascade of coarse powder dusted the bed.

Christine cried out as the discomfort in her head became intensely painful. Strobe lights popped in her eyes as a torrent of images—the *festa*, the *boto*, the man in white, the black water and half-glimpsed towers of green glass—flashed through her mind, and were gone. Christine collapsed back into the pillow.

The hawk-eyed crone whirled on her grandson, pointing at the young woman who lay in bed, blinking back tears and breathing heavily. She once again berated him in that incomprehensible dialect, and his face went pale under his boatman's tan. Bowing his head, he rubbed his eyes with one hand while he mumbled a prayer, or a curse. The old woman began circling the bed, laying down a thin line of powder as she chanted to herself.

"Diogo...what is it? What's going on?" Christine was desperate, afraid; her whole world felt like it was collapsing around her. "Diogo, *what happened to me?*"

"Aaah, Miss Moura, I am so sorry," the boatman began. "I didn't...I didn't think it was possible." He swallowed hard. "It's the *encantado*, Miss Moura, the dolphin-man spirit. He has gotten hold of you somehow.

"This here," he gestured to indicate the granules that were scattered on her bed, "is *manioc* flour. To the *encantado* it is poison, and his magic rejects it; your reaction to it is proof there is a spell on you. I'm sorry, Miss..."

"Wait, Diogo! A magic spell? You're saying that the dolphins cast a *magic spell* on me, and that's why some guy tried to drown me in the river?" Her voice was tinged with hysteria.

Diogo looked as though he was in physical pain. "Please, Miss, I know it's difficult to believe; I didn't really believe it myself. But you must trust me, and you must trust Grandmother. You have to leave this place, now. You must go far away from the river and never come back!"

He reached behind him for the plastic bag that lay on the floor. "Here are all your things I recovered from the riverside, your clothes and your camera and camera bag. I will make arrangements for the rest of your things at the hotel, and make arrangements for the earliest flight out. You mustn't sleep even one more night here, or you will be lost!"

"Lost? Diogo, I can't just..."

"Yes! Yes, you can and you must. You saw the city in the river, didn't you?"

"The city...? How did you...no. No, that was a hallucination, something I dredged up as I blacked out, from the stories you told me."

"It wasn't a hallucination, Miss Moura, and those stories have more truth in them than even I was willing to believe at the time. Your body is weak now, because of what the *encantado* took from you, but your will is still strong, having resisted him once. But you are enchanted, and enchanted you will remain. You will not be able to resist a second time; the City, the *Encante*, will call you back. Your only hope is to go far away. Leave, tonight. *Please.*"

She saw the full terror of total belief in his eyes, and thought about New York. After all that had happened, she thought, didn't it make more sense just to leave? She got what she came for, and under the circumstances her editor couldn't begrudge a couple hundred bucks of extra airfare if she moved her departure up a few days. Magic spells and evil spirits notwithstanding, the idea of getting out of Manaus was more appealing than any of her other options.

"OK, Diogo. I'll leave as soon as I can get a flight. You'll take care of it?"

"Yes, Miss Moura, of course!" The stocky Brazilian's relief was obvious. "There is a charter flight out to Sao Paulo this evening, and I will get you on it. You should stay here and rest now, but try not to sleep. I will come for you when everything is taken care of."

After he'd gone, taking his grandmother with him, Christine opened up the plastic bag he'd left at her feet. Her camera was there, undamaged, and her bag, and her clothes. There was also something she didn't recognize, a handkerchief of shimmering blue-green cloth. She pulled it out to get a better look.

It was cool to the touch, and it flowed over her hands like water. It was the finest piece of silk she'd ever handled. There was a mild stain in one corner that smelled slightly of sugarcane liquor; it was all somehow familiar and comforting. She held it in her hands, turning it over and over as she lay back in bed and tried to put her thoughts in order, listening to the sound of rain rushing like a river outside her window.

Soon she fell into a deep sleep. She didn't even wake up when one of the nurses, clucking her tongue in annoyance, came in to sweep up the mess of flour someone had carelessly spilled on the floor.

The towers of her City rose up around her as she walked, in glittering canyons of glass and stone. Broad cobblestone streets carried currents of streaming people, the green glow of the crystal spires casting rippling patterns of light on their smiling faces. In the City it was always twilight. Bright stalls offered treasures and pleasures, good food and intricate jewelry, as musicians and children played on the sidewalks. It was a good place, and she'd spent her entire life here; this was her one and only home.

She didn't take time to stop and sample the City's riches today. There'd be time for that later. Today she had to go down to the water, the cool water where her true love waited for her. She felt the silk cloth in her hand, the token he'd given her to remember him by, and smiled. She could feel him calling her, and she picked up her pace. The walled streets ended as the countless towers of the City gave way to a densely wooded park. Here there were meandering paths and hidden streams, secret groves where lovers could walk in the soft light of the lamps and lanterns that adorned the trees. There'd be time for that later too.

At last she emerged from the woods and came onto the wide promenade that followed the shores of the island that was the City. She could smell the living water, hear it lapping against the stone of the sea wall.

She started running then, out onto a pier that pushed far into the gentle waves. As she ran, she thought she heard someone calling her, and for a moment the world seemed to flicker and spin. But still she kept on, not looking back; the only important thing was her lover, answering his call, being with him where he waited in the water at the end of the pier.

And then, there he was. His pale skin seemed to glow in the black water where he floated, and his dark eyes caught and held her. He wasn't alone. Around him were others, his friends and companions—her friends and companions now too. She couldn't see them as she stood trembling with love and excitement at the end of that long finger of stone, but she knew they were there.

Again she thought she heard another voice calling her, and again the City seemed to ripple and change, making her head spin. She tried to ignore it, clutching her lover's square of green silk for strength, but once more the voice came and she hesitated, toes at the edge of the stone. For a moment, something seemed wrong with the world, with the water.

In her mind she felt her lover's call with renewed urgency. *Now*, he called from the rippling blackness in which he floated. *You must come now!* As the others echoed his entreaty, the City regained its stability—the water shone more beautifully then ever, the stone was solid beneath her feet and the only place she belonged was with *them*, down in the deep. She held the cool silk to her breast and raised her foot to take that single, perfect step.

And, in a searing white flash, her world exploded.

When her senses returned, the City was gone. She was sprawled back on the wooden planks of a dock jutting out into the river. The stink of the water and the closeness of the humid tropical night surrounded her, and she felt strong hands holding her shoulders. At the end of the half-rotted pier, a little old woman, Diogo's grandmother, stood shouting curses and commands, flinging handfuls of powder from her bag out over the sluggish water.

In the water were dolphins, a great mass of them, scattering away from the woman's repelling dust like oil scatters from a drop of detergent. They dived down, darting away, making an ever-widening circle. But in the center of that circle a single dolphin remained, oblivious to the dust and shouts of the old woman, its bulbous pink head and long beak bobbing on the water, its frightening black eyes fixed on Christine's.

A wave of sadness, a feeling of loss and regret, washed over her, and then it—*he*—was gone, down under the water with a flick of his powerful tail. She knew she could never follow. He was gone, and she was left on the damp boards of the dock, shivering in the heat, weak as a baby. She was still in her hospital gown.

"Miss Moura...it's over. Are you all right?" Diogo held her protectively, afraid to let go. He must have pulled her back from the brink, she thought.

"Yes. Yes, I'll be OK, Diogo. Thank you." The boatman's grandmother glanced back at her, nodded with a satisfied grunt and glared again at the river, fists on her hips.

Remembering, Christine looked down at the soft object she still clutched in her fist: a brown, waterlogged leaf. The silk handkerchief, like the *boto*, was gone. She looked around her. The river was dirty, the air was thick and ripe, insects swarmed and night birds croaked out their harsh cries. But still she felt the magic in it all, the not-so-secret enchantment that lies at the heart of every-thing, if you care to see it. She knew now that never again would the magic of the world be lost to her.

She tossed the soggy leaf out onto the water and watched it drift slowly away through the sparkling dia-monds of the city's reflected light.

"Thank you," she whispered.

The Beast of le Gévaudan

Though every nation of Europe is steeped in tales of humans who take on the aspect of beasts and commit horrible crimes, it would be hard to top France for sheer documented bloodthirstiness. Whether the monster is called loup-garou, bisclaveret *or some other name, the records and chronicles of that country are packed full of cases, not only of fearsome wolf-creatures marauding from the wooded hills of the French countryside, but of men and women who, through madness or witchcraft, have believed themselves to be animals or werewolves. The bloody murders committed by these deranged individuals throughout history are as shockingly numerous as they are gruesome.*

The 16th century was an especially busy time for wolf-men in France, with hundreds of "werewolf" trials being held as panicked citizens attempted to root out the evil they were sure lurked among them. Consider the trial, in 1521, of "Gros Pierre" ("Fat Peter") Burgot and Michel Verdun at the town on Poligny. The pair confessed to having made deals with the Devil in exchange for the powers of the werewolf, and in their years-long rampage across the region they claimed to have killed and consumed dozens of people, mainly children. On the stand, they told fantastic stories of warlocks' sabbaths (i.e., "Black Masses"), human sacrifice, mass murder and lesser perversions, such as mating with she-wolves while in beast form. The two madmen, werewolves or not, were found guilty and duly hanged, along with a third accomplice. Similar events repeated themselves, time after time, all throughout France in the 1500s.

And then there's the story of young Jean Grenier, age 14, who in June of 1603 made a cheerful confession of having prowled the southwest of France with a coven of nine other werewolves, feasting on human flesh—he found small children especially tender and delicious. According to Grenier's tale, he had run away from an abusive father and found himself in the company of an older youth, one Pierre de la Tilhaire. This friend one day invited him to come with him into the woods, where the younger boy would be introduced to a being referred to as "the Lord of the Forest."

This lord, in Grenier's telling, was a huge man in black, riding a black horse of incredible size. Pledging themselves into the dark giant's service, the two boys were given magical wolf-skins and a special ointment that enabled them to travel in the form of wolves. In this way, said Grenier, did he and his friend, along with the lord and a half-dozen other followers, terrorize the countryside. Witnesses corroborated Grenier's accounts of the time, place and manner of his numerous killings, and the boy was judged insane and sentenced to strict confinement at a Franciscan friary. Here he continued in the animal behavior, walking on all fours, growling like a wolf and refusing all food but the foulest scraps of meat.

Was Jean Grenier insane, or genuinely afflicted (or, in his opinion, blessed) with the shapeshifter's curse? Is were-wolfism, lycanthropy, a supernatural condition or a violent mental illness? The more materialist view of psychology and anthropology tends toward the latter. But if this is the case, why such a concentration of wolf-mad killers in France? Perhaps it has much to do with the cultural environment: as the homicidal mania grips the madman, he ascribes his savage new feelings to the werewolfism he'd been raised to believe in, kills and confesses under that delusion and feeds the cycle of clinical lycanthropy. Certainly, no other nation is as rich in accounts of savage child-killing wolf-men lurking outside the door. And few of these accounts are as famous, bloody, twisted and well documented as the strange case of the Beast of le Gévaudan.

Le Gévaudan is a rough, hilly, windswept region of forests and pastures in southern France, approximately 300 kilometers from the city of Lyon. Today it is a largely rural area, but in the 17th century it was a backwater, a hardscrabble land of hardy shepherd-folk. It was these people who, for three long years, had to endure not only the murderous rampages of a seemingly unkillable Beast, but the ruinous presence of the various legions of armed men who were sent to hunt the thing down.

The nightmare began on the first of July 1764, when Jeanne Boulet, of Saint-Étienne de Lugardes, was attacked by a wild animal and torn apart. This kind of attack was not unheard-of, but still somewhat shocking because wolves rarely attacked shepherds; the whole point of a shepherd in the first place was to keep predators away. But it marked the beginning of a killing season that would see more than 15 people, almost all of them young children, dead from animal attacks. The Beast had arrived.

Those unlucky enough to witness an attack by the Beast gave differing descriptions of the thing, but all agreed that it was something more than an ordinary wolf. In October 1764, a Monsieur de Barthe gave a portrait of the Beast as having "a broad head, very large, like that of a calf with the muzzle of a greyhound. The reddish hair is striped with black on the back and the breast is tinged with gray. The front legs are short, the tail extraordinarily broad and long. When it stalks it lies low, chest to the ground, and crawls: then it does not appear larger than a large fox. When it is near enough to pounce, its springs on its prey and its advance is made in a wink...its size is greater than a large wolf." De Barthe also noted that the Beast seemed to use its claws, not its teeth, when attacking.

Whatever it was, the task of hunting it down fell to a Captain Duhamel and his band of soldiers or dragoons. Headquartering in Saint-Chely d'Apcher, Duhamel organized huge hunts, with hundreds and even thousands of men beating the bushes and fields to drive out the Beast—or beasts—that lurked there. Duhamel and his men succeeded in killing dozens of wolves, but children were still dying on a nearly weekly basis. These massive hunts drained the already weak economy of the region: men were taken from work, precious supplies were consumed, the soldiers were arrogant and antagonized the peasants and their salaries drained the treasuries of the parishes. Eventually the people's anger and frustration forced Duhamel and his men to be recalled to another district.

The new year of 1765 was to be forever known as the Year of Death. Beginning on January 2 with the slaying of 14-year-old Jean de Chateauneuf, there would be over 50 brutal killings before the year was out. The madness of the time can only be imagined: weekly deaths, mainly of small children; soldiers and horsemen riding and shooting all over the countryside; wool production and farming brought to a standstill, and through it all stalked the shadow of the unkillable Beast. Every tactic one can imagine was tried to *bring the Beast in: huge hunts of 20,000 men or more, small hunting parties with dogs and sharpshooters, traps, poison, prayers—you name it.*

The next Beast-slayer to jump into this mess after the reassignment of Captain Duhamel was the famous Norman wolf-hunter, Denneval d'Alencon, dispatched to le Gévaudan by order of the king. He and his son, a regimental captain, arrived with six proven bloodhounds, a reputation for having killed over 12,000 wolves in his long career and a confident attitude. That attitude would prove to be mis-placed. By the end of July, Denneval and son would be gone from le Gévaudan, having sunk into despair and drink as the peasantry grumbled against them and the blood contin-ued to flow in the hills.

Replacing the failed Denneval—though originally they were meant to work together—was King Louis XV's own Master of the Hunt, Antoine de Beauterne, who arrived in the region in mid-June of 1765. Antoine's methods were the polar opposite of Denneval's huge bush-beatings, which would often cover 50 parishes or more. The king's huntsman was more subtle, more inclined to rely on careful study of the pattern of attacks in an attempt to guess the Beast's habits and be ready with marksmen when it showed itself. Though his methods were less disruptive, the weary peasants of the region still resented his presence and continued lack of results, and the popular press in Paris and Lyon was filled with sensationalistic accounts of the depredations of the Beast. Antoine was under intense pressure from the king to show results. On September 21, he did.

The kill took place in an apple-orchard attached to the royal abbey of Chazes, where the Beast had been reported seen four days earlier. Antoine arrived at the abbey with 40 gunners drawn from the adjoining parishes and set up a series of ambushes at key points. Men and dogs then beat forward into the grove in a steady line, in hopes of driving the Beast toward the waiting guns. It was Antoine himself who scored the first shot on the thing that emerged from the trees, taking it in the shoulder. His man Rinchard finished it off with a second shot, when it was but 10 feet from the master huntsman.

Antoine wasted no time in declaring the Beast dead, having several witnesses who survived the Beast's attacks swear that this was, indeed, the thing they had faced. Antoine sent the enormous black carcass, stuffed and mounted, back to the royal court where his wife wrote, in a gushing letter, "The king [did] nothing but speak about that all the day!" Antoine de Beauterne was awarded the honor of the Cross of Saint-Louis, an astounding 1000-livre bump to his pension and was granted the right to place the Beast of le Gévaudan upon his coat of arms. The huntsman was a hero, and for a while it seemed the nightmare was over.

In March 1766 that began to change with the wolf-killing of Jean Bourgougnoux of Montchauvet. There were only six more deaths from wild animal attacks that year, more than would occur in a normal year, and far more than one would expect in a district where lately tens of thousands of men had for nearly two years been busy emptying the forests and hills of wolves. The people began to whisper. When 13 bloody killings took place in the first five months of 1667, the people began to panic. The authorities in Paris sent no troops this time, only kegs of wolf-poison. How could they do otherwise, having just made Antoine de Beauterne a hero for ending the very problem that oppressed the peasants?

It was up to a local lord, the Marquis d'Apcher, to step into the role that had belonged to Duhamel, Denneval and Antoine. Only 19 years old, the young aristocrat was popular with the people of the area and organized several hunting parties to track down the newly resurrected Beast. At last, on June 19, they had their kill. One of his huntsmen, Jean Chastel, who had been thrown in prison along with his sons during Antoine's time in le Gévaudan, had been sitting apart from the rest of his group of hunters, praying. It was then that the Beast appeared, stalking out of the trees. Chastel, sure that the Virgin would protect him, calmly finished his prayer before shooting the thing dead.

These are the facts of the story, or at least a version of them, and as many as can be dealt with in a single story in this book—controversies still swirl over exactly what was going on in le Gévaudan, and the detailed records of the time are extensive enough to fill a hefty encyclopedia. As with all things, we must pick and choose. The following accounts are fictional but based on facts, stories of that blood-soaked place, that terrible time when men, women and children fought desperately against the unknown, unkillable Beast...

November 1764

Pierre de Chateauneuf sat staring in the single room of his tiny stone hovel, shivering beside the slowly dying fire that glowed in the hearth. His hands, folded on his lap, were red with frostbite, but Pierre was numb to the pain. He could feel nothing now but grief; outside, wrapped in a roughly woven sheet now stained with blood, in the heart of the wild snowstorm that had raged for two days through the isolated French hill country of le Gévaudan, was the maimed and mangled body of 15-year-old Jean de Chateauneuf, his only son.

Why did I let him go out there? Pierre knew the answer to his question as soon as he asked it of himself, every time he asked it; they were shepherds, and there were sheep to tend. Snowstorm or no snowstorm, work had to be done and Jean had gone to do it. When he hadn't come back on the first night, Pierre was concerned but not overly worried. His son knew the country and how to survive in it; it wouldn't be the first time hard weather had forced him to sleep rough. But when a second day passed with no sign of Jean or their flock, Pierre knew something was wrong. Wrapping himself in a heavy sheepskin coat to ward off the storm's icy blasts, he'd left the safety of the farmstead to search for his missing son.

How long he trudged through that howling white hell, shouting Jean's name above the fury of the winds, he couldn't remember. His hands and feet went numb as the hours passed, his voice hoarse and cracked from calling through the storm. At last, blinded by the driving snow, he'd heard the faint bleating of a frightened sheep. Following the cry, he came upon the remnants of his flock, terrified and half-frozen on the hillside, surrounded by the torn and bloody carcasses of those sheep that hadn't been lucky enough to survive. *Wolves*, Pierre had first thought, *driven down into the valley by the hunger of winter.* But if the flock was here, where was Jean?

It was then that one of the snow-covered shapes caught his eye, a red-stained mass he'd at first assumed was another of his slaughtered sheep. As he approached it through the white veil of the snowstorm, the sickening realization came to him—this was no animal, but his own son, slashed and gutted and left for dead on the frozen slope of the valley. A day's snowfall had covered any tracks, but it was clear to Pierre, even in his frantic state, that the attacking creature was no ordinary wolf.

The depth of the gaping wounds on his son's body, the size of the jaws that must have made those bites and tears, the sheer violence of the slaughter—it was unthinkable. There had been a great many wolf attacks in the region this year, and his neighbors had begun whispering that there was a *loup-garou*, a werewolf in their midst, but Pierre had scoffed at their panic until he saw the thing's gruesome work with his own eyes. His grief was laced with cold threads of fear as he dragged his son's body home through the howling storm.

And now he sat, staring at the fire in his empty stone hovel, left alone and childless like so many others by the Beast that stalked the forested valleys of le Gévaudan. How many had died since that summer when the attacks began? Dozens? Almost every week, there had been word of another death or maiming: a young shepherd girl of Rieutort de Randon, torn apart by a huge animal not 50 yards from her front door as her mother and brother looked on; a 10-year-old of Bergounhoux badly wounded in the face before her brothers drove the Beast off with their makeshift spears.

And now, thought Pierre as the sharp sting of feeling crept cruelly back into his frozen fingers, my fine young Jean must be added to the list.

The dying fire glowed red and the winter chill invaded the room; Pierre moved to stir the embers and place another branch into the hearth. Bending to pick up the poker, he suddenly froze as his ears, still alert with the adrenaline of the last few hours, caught a scrabbling, scratching sound coming from outside the shuttered window, above the whine of the blizzard. For long seconds he hung there, half crouched, waiting for the noise to repeat itself. A windblown branch, maybe, or a stray sheep? Or maybe, Pierre thought, it was just some wild animal. He quickly corrected himself, his mind racing with thoughts of his son and the Beast in the hills.

No, he thought. *No, there can be no such thing as "just" a wild animal. Not in le Gévaudan, not anymore.*

There! The sound came again, a slow, sharp dragging across the wood of the shutters and the stone of the hovel's walls. Claws? Pierre thought of his son's horrible wounds, long red furrows against white skin. Ever so slowly, he began to inch toward the loaded flintlock musket that leaned against the doorframe. With each new noise, every skritch and scuffle from outside, he would go still again until, after what seemed like an eternity of silently crossing the red-dark room, his fingers found the familiar weight of his dependable old weapon. Cradling the gun, he moved like a hunter across the dim room, finally reaching the wood-covered window. Pausing first to say a silent prayer, his right hand gripping the gun with finger on the trigger, he reached out with his left and flung open the shutter.

The sight that confronted him was out of nightmare, the face of a creature from Hell. A gleaming snarl of ivory fangs surrounded by a hideously wolfish muzzle of dark fur rose toward him with a heartstopping animal cry, a vision of pure animal death that caused the terrified shepherd to leap backward, falling on his back, shouting incoherently. And those eyes—the Beast's huge, rolling eyes were alive with bloodlust and a frightening intelligence. Pierre had faced wolves before, and looked into their eyes, and this was no ordinary wolf; in those eyes was reflected a malevolent consciousness, the soul of a creature that loved killing for killing's sake.

Something broke free inside Pierre as his gaze locked with that of the snarling Beast lunging through the window, and his panic and terror were replaced by a hatred stronger than both. This was an unnatural creature, an abomination; he knew then that he was looking into the face of Satan, a thing of pure evil, and his humanity screamed against it. With his righteous hatred came clarity, and the shepherd's hand shot out for the musket he'd dropped in his fall. In one swift motion, he swung the long gun up from the hovel's dirt floor and trained it on the thing in the window. His finger twitched, and the tiny stone cabin cracked with the deafening thunder of black powder.

The toothy bulk of the Beast disappeared from the window with a soul-tearing howl, but Pierre's hunter's instincts told him the shot had gone wide even before he heard the thing howl once more, and heard the sound of animal footsteps in the snow. By that time, the shepherd

was already reloading his weapon, a process which would normally take a skilled musketeer 20 seconds or so; driven by anger and pure adrenaline, Pierre did it in less than 15. Gripping his musket tightly, he kicked open the farmhouse door to face the Beast outside, the thing that had killed his boy.

Though the wind still tore through the valley, the snow had dwindled greatly, and Pierre's keen eyes, adjusted to the dim light since his little fire had died down, quickly made out the shaggy shape, already halfway across the farmyard and headed swiftly for the cover of the brush, and the wooded hills beyond. *Mother of God*, he thought. *It's huge!* Bigger than any wolf he'd seen, with longer legs, it loped across the snow-covered ground in long, reaching strides that ate up the distance at an amazing rate. Pierre raised his gun once more, but held little hope of hitting the retreating beast. A musket is difficult to aim at the best of times, but at this distance, against a moving target, it would take a miracle. The shepherd whispered a plea for exactly that, and tugged the trigger.

The gun's booming report echoed in the valley as the Beast disappeared into the undergrowth at the edge of the field. Without thinking Pierre began the reflexive motions of reloading the firearm, fully intending to go after the murderous creature, to hunt it down, to kill it and end its reign of terror, to have its foul hide for a rug, to hang its skull above his fireplace, but his rage slipped from him as quickly as it had come. The powder horn tumbled from his trembling fingers, and his musket fell to the half-frozen earth.

To go after the Beast would be death, of that he was certain. He could feel the thing out there in the trees, in its own domain, watching him, mocking him, waiting for him. Standing there in the yard of his tiny farmstead, with the shrouded body of his only son at his feet and the winter wind cutting him as it screamed through the remote French hill country, Pierre de Chateauneuf looked out at the vast, dark forest and wept.

God help us, he prayed. *God help us all.*

Late December 1764

"...and deliver us from evil. Amen."

The Bishop of Mende crossed himself and rose from the floor where he'd knelt in prayer. Heavy rings on plump fingers gleamed in the firelight that filled the bishop's sumptuous study—even here in the backwoods of France, men of the Church lived in style—but the bishop was not a contented man. These were trying times; a plague of death was upon the land, and the people needed proper instruction and guidance. Already, there was too much dangerous superstition and error running around.

The old clergyman sighed as he walked with heavy steps back to his grand oak desk, where notes for his New Year message to his flock were scattered among letters and records of killings, disasters, animal attacks and dozens of incredible descriptions of the marauding Beast. The bishop was not so distant from the people that he wasn't well aware of the wild responses this year of blood had provoked: all through the hill country there was talk of demons walking the land, of witchcraft and werewolves, magic spells, curses and the *loup-garou*. There was even a large consensus that the Beast was Satan himself, the Adversary walking the land, free and unbound from Hell!

And of course, in this environment of superstition and fear, there was no shortage of evil men profiting through the sale of charms, potions, talismans and "magic spells," all guaranteed to keep the Beast away.

Witchcraft! Idolatry and witchcraft! The bishop's blood boiled as he thought of it, this pagan madness coursing unchecked through his domain. If there were demons from Hell loose in le Gévaudan, if there was a curse on the land, if the Deceiver had been given leave to wander France causing confusion and calamity, it was because the Lord God had willed it to be so! For an otherwise good man to turn to the lies of sorcerers and wizards to protect himself in his fear was surely as damning as witchcraft performed with evil intent; to acknowledge and attempt to appease a power greater than God was a mortal error. The only proper response in this time of trial was prayer and repentance, obedience and humility toward God. Yes, it is right that the people should fear—they should fear the anger of the Almighty! For the sake of their immortal souls, they had to be corrected.

Flushed with zeal and righteous wrath, the bishop picked up his pen once more. Devastating wars, crop-killing falls of hail, ruinous livestock mortality and the killing storms which have "deprived the ploughman of his bread," he wrote, were "a mark of the anger of God against this country.

"And now a savage animal, unknown to this region, appears suddenly as if by miracle, leaving everywhere bloody traces of its cruelty. Through stealth and trickery, this man-eating Beast pounces on its victims with incredible speed. It appears in various places, very distant from each other, and its preferred victims are children of the most tender age, and the weaker sex.

"Is not the Bible filled with examples of animals sent by God to punish humanity?" the bishop asked, warming to his point with gruesome examples. "The snakes of the time of Moses, the bears the avenged Elijah by devouring the 42 children that had made fun of him, the lion which killed the guilty messenger that withheld information from Jeroboam?

"As for this Beast," the bishop continued, imagining his sermon thundering out in churches throughout the region, "I say it is the wrathful Lord who sent it against you! It carries out the death sentence of divine justice. If it kills your children, isn't this because you raise them badly, in ambition, pride and contempt for the poor?"

The monsignor next targeted the youth, young women especially, whose immodesty and lustfulness called the plague of the Beast down upon themselves. Their "criminal and idolatrous flesh, used as a tool of the Devil to lure hearts and souls, and thus deserved to be delivered to the fatal teeth of savage beasts." In pointing out the grievous sin of women and youth, though, the bishop was careful to note that he wasn't letting the rest of the people off lightly. This iniquity and godlessness, he wrote, was general and pervasive.

But however terrible the Beast might be, he advised, it was not invulnerable to iron and fire. "It will die," he wrote, "under some huntsman's blows, as soon as God wishes it to die." To hasten this moment of divine mercy, all churches were commanded to hold prayer vigils on three consecutive Sundays, to repent and beg God's forgiveness.

After he had finished writing, the old bishop leaned back and reread his letter, satisfied with his work. It put the blame and responsibility for this calamity squarely where it belonged, on the shoulders and souls of sinful humanity. *Only hard trials like these can bring a fallen-away people back to God*, the weary cleric thought, pouring a cup of wine in the warm firelight.

"A new beginning for a New Year," he toasted aloud. Sipping the wine and gazing into the flames, he added a silently bitter afterthought—*at least it can't get any worse.*

It was December 1764, and the good Bishop of Mende had no idea how wrong the year 1765 would prove him to be.

January 1765

"Captain! Hey, Captain Duhamel!"

The middle-aged dragoon commander, grizzled and weather-beaten before his time by years of the professional soldier's life, turned and scowled as he heard his name called, seeing his second-in-command making his way across the tavern's crowded common room. Here in the bustle of the little inn of the town of Mende, Duhamel had hoped to have a drink and some time to himself, a break from the nonstop madness his job had become. He'd never imagined that a post like commanding a force of guardsmen in a sleepy backwater would make him long for the relative peace and quiet of open warfare, but that was before he'd become the chief wolf-hunter in a neighborhood overrun with wolves. *Maybe I should take vows*, he thought bitterly, *and follow my cousin into the monastery.*

Before he could indulge his fantasies of monkhood further, his second was straddling a chair beside him. "So, captain," the younger soldier grinned with the black humor of the professional fighting man, "have you been saying your prayers like a good boy?"

"Gah! Do you have to bring that up?" Duhamel pressed his finger to his aching temples. "It's bad enough fighting an entire army of wolves, trying to get the peasants to cooperate with us while their children and neighbors are getting eaten alive every other day. Now it's a holy plague from God we're fighting? Great!"

"Ah! You've heard the bishop's New Year's message, then?" the other man asked, teasing.

"How could I not? The priests read it at every mass now. I especially like the part about how some great hunter's going to kill the thing just as soon as God wills it. Now they expect some kind of holy warrior, and I hate to break it to you, *mon ami*, but the last time I looked in the barracks there weren't a lot of knights in shining armor to be found."

Duhamel paused to spit into the fire and drain his wine cup. "But maybe," he continued in a dry tone, "the old fellow is right. Maybe his brilliant plan will reduce the number of attacks; if everyone's inside the church praying, they won't be wandering around the countryside getting themselves killed."

His officer's smile faded, as he lowered his voice to reply. "I wouldn't place any bets on that, boss."

All trace of humor left the captain. "What? Another one? What happened?"

"Two days ago, captain," the soldier replied, "on the 28th, near Aumont."

"Lord! So close?"

"Yeah. A 12-year-old girl this time, all chewed up while she tended the cattle. She'll probably live, I'm told; her brother heard her screams and put up a real fight. Apparently the cows got a couple good horn hits in too, before the Beast headed for the hills."

"*Mon dieu!*" Duhamel pounded on the table with his fist, and several pairs of eyes turned their way, easily guessing what his outburst had been about. The captain glowered darkly at them until they wisely turned their attention back to their drinks. "How many is that now?"

"In the past few weeks? Let me think." The soldier counted off on his fingers. "End of November, there was that old lady that was killed tending her cow; you remember, that was the one where we left the body lying out for three days in the hope the Beast would come back for its kill so we could ambush it?" The younger man caught the nasty look from his captain and quickly continued ticking off his tally of slaughter.

"Before that there was that shepherd's boy, and on the 15th, there was that 45-year-old woman in Vedrines, Catherine Chastang. They found her head a hundred yards away from her body, I'm told. Then on the 21st there was that girl who was mauled around the head. Again, we left the body and waited in ambush, but..."

"Yes, enough! I remember." Duhamel paused with his head in his hands. "So which Beast showed up this time?" he muttered into his palms. "The red-necked Beast that walks on two legs? The bear-like Beast with arms like a monkey? The one that starts out tiny, like a little dog, but then grows to the size of a horse?"

"Ah, no sir," the officer replied, the grin slowly creeping back onto his face and into his voice. "Our humble province, it seems, has been blessed by yet another visitor from Hell. This one, she's as big as a bull, with front legs like a bear, a long body like a leopard and a tail as thick as your arm!"

Duhamel sat silently for a long time, staring at the floor. When at last he spoke there was exhaustion, and a frightening hint of despair, in his voice. "We've been hunting for months, lieutenant. We've beaten down the forests, we've flushed out the fields, we've put hundreds of men and scores of horses into every corner of these damned mountains, and how many wolves have we killed? How many, lieutenant?"

"Seventy, sir, give or take," the lieutenant replied, quietly.

"Seventy," growled Duhamel, with a savagely ironic grin. "Seventy wolves! In less than three months! Have you ever heard of such a thing, of such a feat of wolf-hunting?"

"No sir." The younger man's voice was almost a whisper. "No, I haven't."

"No," sighed Duhamel, subsiding and slumping into his chair. "Neither have I. And still they come, and still women and children die. I imagine them pouring out of a hole in the ground, *mon ami*. I see a gateway to Hell somewhere in the mountains, and all these wolves pouring out of it like ground flour pouring out of a mill."

"That's an easy vision to believe, sir," his officer replied.

Captain Duhamel stared into the fire, listening to the clatter and chatter of the inn around him. "I don't know what to do, boy," he said. "I don't know whether to pray or get drunk."

"We're soldiers, old man, practical people," answered the lieutenant, clapping his captain on the back with one hand while signaling the innkeeper for more wine with the other. "There's no reason we can't do both."

January 12, 1765

The young soldier screamed in the freezing rain and rushed forward with his lance, swinging the bladed tip upward in a wild arc meant to rip the belly of his opponent. His fierce charge was followed up by a half-dozen vicious downward thrusts meant to finish off the monstrous enemy as it lie prone on the ground. The deed done, he leaned heavily on his long spear, resting from the exertion of battle.

"*That*," he said at last as he straightened and pulled his weapon out of the sticking winter mud, "is what I'd do if the Beast shows up around here."

Jacques-Andre Portefaix, age 12, grinned at his younger cousin's display of spearmanship. Even at the tender age of eight years, young Jacques Panafieu's head was already full of hundreds of imagined military triumphs. The presence of the Beast in the countryside had only served to give him one more focus for his dreams of combat glory; now he was a mighty hunter, single-handedly bringing down the *loup-garou* when thousands of men had failed.

Portefaix couldn't resist teasing his warlike little cousin. "Well, that was pretty good, Jacques," he drawled, "but your charge was too wasteful! You've got to come down from above, put your weight into it. Let the spear do the work! At your size, you'd need all the help you could get to stab through the Beast's thick hide."

The other shepherd children gathered around joined in his laughter as the boy went red in the face. It was so easy to bait the short but stocky farmboy—he took everything so seriously. Scowling, he spat on the ground and gave an angry shrug in perfect imitation of his father.

"Ah, what do you know, idiot?" he snapped. "Stabbing down's no good. There's too much bone in the way. You've got to get at the underbelly or neck, or the rear flank where you can get past the ribs!"

"All right, all right," Portefaix said, after the new round of laughter had died down. "Whatever you say, Captain. Now keep an eye on those sheep; if the Beast shows up, you won't get a chance to use your techniques if your back is turned, eh?"

Spitting again, the scrappy little rooster turned away from his cousin to sulk, gripping his crude spear tightly and scowling at the grazing animals. The children's laughter died in the dampness, their moment of fun passing as they remembered why they were there and returned to watchful silence. Most of the sheep of their village of Villeret had been gathered into this one big flock in hopes that strength of numbers might deter the Beast or beasts, whichever was responsible for the continuing killings of people and livestock in the region. There were five other young shepherds watching the mass of sheep besides Portefaix and his cousin: Jacques Couston and Jean Pic, both 12 years old; nine-year-old girls Jeanne Gueffier and Madeline Chausse; and Jean Veyrier, another eight-year-old boy.

As the biggest of the boys, and the oldest by a few months, Portefaix was the acknowledged leader of their little band, but he wasn't glad of it. He looked at the "spears" they had been given—little more than long sticks with crude knife-blades lashed to the ends—and wondered what they could possibly do to the unkillable Beast if it came for the livestock. Nothing, probably. But he'd been instructed on how to arrange his small spearmen should they have to fight, and had done his best to drill them in the proper formations. They were as ready as a half-dozen frightened children could ever be.

He shivered, and not from his morbid thoughts; the weather was miserable. A cold, misty rain fell constantly, drenching everything and chilling the bones; this rain combined with a thaw to turn the hillside pasture into an expanse of frigid, squelching mud. Some parts of the pasture were in fact full-fledged mud pits, and care had to be taken to keep the sheep away from these sucking bogs. Pulling a frightened sheep out of knee-high muck in a freezing January rain was the last thing Jacques-Andre Portefaix wanted to do.

Make that the second-last thing, he corrected himself, thinking once more of the Beast that was roaming the hills and woods. *But would even a monster be out in damned weather like this?*

It was then that the first worried bleatings came from the flock, as if taking their cue from the shepherds' worst fears. The sheep began to mill about, restless and nervous; they smelled or heard something they didn't like. If there's one thing the children had learned early, it was to never ignore the instincts of sheep. Portefaix and the other older boys exchanged quick, frightened glances and brought their weapons to the ready, as little Panafieu's head snapped up to attention and the other young shepherds gripped their spears with white knuckles. The tension of the moment hung there, filled with the white noise of rain and the warning sound of agitated sheep.

And then the Beast was upon them.

From a thicket less than 50 yards away it exploded, with a savage roar that was almost a scream. It was an enormous creature, bigger, it seemed, than any wolf they'd seen or dreamed of seeing. A boiling mass of fur and fangs sped toward them on impossibly fast legs. Fear washed over young Portefaix as he watched that vision of violent death storm down on them, but somehow protective instincts and the responsibility of leadership kept his head clear as he shouted out commands to his terrified band of defenders.

"Form up! Form up!" he cried as he rushed to form a bristling front line of spears with Couston and Pic. "Remember what I told you!"

The Beast ignored the bleating flock, which was now scattering in panic; its target was the flock's human guardians. The children could see the hate and hunger in its bestial face as it closed the distance with its huge strides. Portefaix and the boys in the front rank braced themselves for the thing's headlong charge, ready to strike at the Beast's underbelly as it leaped upon them.

But the snarling creature was smarter than to throw itself onto their fence of iron knife-blades; at the last minute, just when the clash seemed inevitable, it darted off to the side and wheeled around to the little battalion's unprotected flank. The young shepherds desperately tried to turn their defense to meet the thing's attack, but before their clumsy weapons could be brought into play, the white-fanged Beast was in the air, snarling, plunging for the throat of their smallest member—little Jacques Panafieu.

The farmboy screamed as the huge creature's weight bore him down to the mud, an unstoppable avalanche of stinking wet fur and dripping jaws. The Beast lunged for Jacques' unprotected face and neck, taking a savage bite out of his cheek as the other shepherds stabbed at the animal in terrified frenzy. Their unskilled attacks and their makeshift spears couldn't pierce the thick hide of the Beast, but the sheer volume of wild stabs, screams and shouts quickly drove it back off the fallen boy. The children watched in horror as it sprang away with a bloody piece of their friend's face in its jaws. It circled around them a few paces away as it enjoyed the morsel, licking its red-stained jaws and growling like rolling thunder all the while, staring at them with hate-filled eyes.

It was far larger than any wolf Jacques Portefaix had seen, far larger than he'd imagined any wolf could be. Easily the size of a yearling calf, it stalked in a menacing crouched posture, its long front legs giving it a look of almost standing erect. Its dark, dense fur was reddish-brown streaked with black, and its massive head was broad and stout, showing those hellish teeth in a wide line. The Beast snorted and snapped in the chill misty rain, waiting for an opening in the shaky line of little spears the shepherds presented; they could smell its wet animal musk as it paced around them, could hear its snarls growing more furious with each long stride.

Then, with that same horrible screaming roar, it launched itself upon them once more, springing low and to the side, under the bristling row of spearpoints. Its target this time was the other young boy, Jean Veyrier. Before the others could make an effective defense, the Beast had snapped its huge jaws on the boy's arm, and the momentum of its pounce had carried it several feet away from the terrified cluster of children. Its teeth sinking deep, it began to drag the hysterical Veyrier away with savage tugs that tore at the child's trapped limb.

"Dog! Motherless dog! I'll send you back to Hell!"

A savage string of imaginative curses sounded behind Portefaix, and he momentarily turned his attention from the slowly retreating Beast to see Panafieu, covered in mud and blood, slogging forward through the muck with his spear held ready. His cheek was one bloody wound, and his voice was slurred from the damage, but the scrappy little shepherd's eyes blazed. He was ready to fight.

"Go around to the right!" Portefaix shouted to Panafieu; he had an idea. "Get around the other side of it! Pic, Madeline, go with him! We'll try to drive it down to that mud-pit!" If that sucking ooze could trap a grown sheep, he figured, maybe it could slow down the Beast enough that even their inexpert spears could get in a killing blow. They had to do it fast, though; Veyrier couldn't survive much more of the punishment he was getting from the Beast's dragging.

"Wh...why don't we just let it go?" asked the other 12-year-old, Couston, in a wavering voice. "It's got...it's got what it wanted. We should let it leave, and be thankful that six of us are still alive. We can't fight that thing, Jacques-Andre! We'll all be killed!"

"No!" Portefaix shouted. "No. We're not letting that Beast have even one of us without a fight. We're shepherds, but now I'm a shepherd of shepherds and I don't plan on losing a single member of my flock! Now let's go; start making noise!"

With shouts, curses, whistles and the clattering of weapons, the small army began its maneuver, circling around three sides of the evil wolf-monster. Couston had been right; the Beast had what it came for, and all it wanted now was to get away and enjoy its sinister meal. Portefaix's tactic left it only one way to make its escape, straight through the gluey basin of sticky winter mud. Dragging its limp victim by the arm, the growling Beast retreated, never taking those hellish eyes off the encircling line of shouting children.

Foot by foot it entered the trap, the mud getting deeper, sucking at its great clawed feet. Veyrier by this time had become dead weight, either unconscious or worse, and his body was like an anchor dragging the Beast to a near-standstill. At last, realizing it could retreat no further, the man-eating terror released the arm of its victim and, standing over the child's unmoving body, made its stand against the young shepherds.

Seeing that the Beast would not proceed, and had unclamped its jaws from Veyrier's limb, Portefaix shouted for his little band of spearmen to advance and attack. At the relatively firm edge of the mudpit they stood in a semicircle, just at the limit of their weapons' range, and began to stab at the Beast.

"The head!" Portefaix called out. "Go for the head, the eyes, the mouth! Even if we can't kill it, we can hurt it!"

The crude spears struck at the Beast in a flurry, stabbing at the thing's broad face and neck as it growled and screamed in frustration. Trapped as much by its unwillingness to give up its delicious catch as by the cold mud of the pasture, it would not get near enough to counterattack. After dozens of blows had landed around its head, it was Portefaix that finally managed to score a solid strike, a bone-crunching blow beneath one yellow eye that left the blade of his spear sitting crooked on its shaft.

That did it. With a yowl of pain, the Beast sprung back from Veyrier, landing even deeper in the muck. Filled with rage and made brave by desperation, Portefaix took the opening and leaped forward with even louder screams and yells, swinging and striking at the air with his now-useless spear. Snarling and spitting, the huge wolf-thing made one last hateful glare at the screaming gang of young shepherds before turning and bolting off with an angry roar.

As the Beast cleared the edge of the mudpit's far side, the shouting of the children turned to cheers as they pelted it with rocks and stones until it was out of range, disappearing up into the thickets of the hillside. When it was gone, Portefaix knelt in the mud to examine the bloody form of Veyrier, and found the boy unconscious but alive. With a whispered prayer of thanks, the young leader closed his eyes and slumped down, uncaring, into the muck, exhausted.

He could hear the faint shouts coming up from the valley far below, people alerted by the shouting up in the hills. Soon there would be men and dogs trying to pick up the trail, to track the thing through the dark winter woods. Portefaix could hear Panafieu crowing:

"Ha! We beat it! We beat that Beast back to Hell! What did I tell you, eh? Strike downward! Go for the head!"

July 1765

Denneval d'Alencon, master wolf-hunter, the proud old Norman who had boasted 12,000 kills in ridding the countryside of predators, took a sloppy guzzle of his wine and gazed sourly across the table at the richly dressed man who sat opposite him. He'd just been given bad news which was also, in its way, very good news. He'd have to drink on it for a while.

"So that's it, then?"

"That's it." Antoine de Beauterne, the king's own Master of the Hunt, looked right back at the bearded old hunter, clearly not liking what he saw. "It's not like you've been doing much lately, anyway, Denneval. A couple of disorganized bush-beatings with no results, a lot of torn-up countryside and angry peasants. You're making trouble for everyone, including His Majesty and myself. You've been paid; you can just as easily drink elsewhere."

Denneval snorted through his grizzled beard. "Yes, I suppose I can. Somewhere less godforsaken, somewhere that isn't plagued by an animal from Hell."

"That animal was the problem you were supposed to take care of."

"Take care of it how? I've gathered hunts, huge beat-ings of thousands of men, lines of hunters and dogs so long you couldn't see one end from the other. I've pulled more wolf-carcasses out of these cursed hills than I'd have once thought possible, and still these peasant brats keep dying."

He took another huge gulp of wine, further staining his beard before continuing. "No, the Beast is unkillable. Either that, or there is a line of Beasts-in-waiting, one stepping forward when the one in front of it dies."

"That's what I'm told Captain Duhamel said before he was reassigned."

"Yes, and I mocked him then as you mock me now. Mocked his methods as you mock mine—though you chide me for going too far where I chided him for not going far enough. But I learned, and you'll learn too, if you stay in this hellhole long enough. The Beast can't be killed."

A strange look passed over Antoine's face. "I never imagined I'd hear the great Duhamel speak of a thing that can't be killed."

The old hunter almost smiled. "Neither did I. But I say it now."

Antoine sighed and looked up at the ceiling of open beams and smoke-stained plaster, rocking back on his rough chair. "Well. Be that as it may, I at least will keep trying. *Somebody* has to kill it. This business is getting out of hand—you've had over half a year, and Duhamel the same before that, and during that time everything's gone to hell. The whole district is being ruined financially, the people are on the point of revolt and—as you say, and lest we forget—peasant children keep dying. The king wants this ended, and I'm going to end it."

The half-drunk old Norman looked as steadily as he could into the younger man's eyes. After a while, he nodded and looked down into the dregs at the bottom of his cup. "Huh. So what's your plan? Still sticking with smaller parties?"

"The other way didn't seem to work, did it? We'll keep tracking the Beast, learning its patterns, and one day— one day soon—we'll be there waiting for it when it shows its ugly face. It's an animal, Denneval, nothing more, and animals are creatures of habit. Besides, nobody's showed me a better plan."

"But plenty of worse ones, eh?" Denneval smirked through his beard.

"My God, yes. Most either suggest painting the entire district with poison, or sending every man, woman and child in le Gévaudan to a monastery or convent, to pray to God to release the land. One man keeps insisting that, since the Beast seems partial to children and females, we make artificial girls out of poisoned pork and set them as decoys across the countryside."

Denneval laughed. "Hah! I remember that fellow. I think there's something wrong in his head. So you really think you're the one, eh? Come out from Paris to bag the Beast?"

"I didn't get to be the King's huntsman by sitting in Paris and playing parlor games, Denneval."

Bitterness flooded into the old man's voice. "Oh? I'd heard differently."

Antoine glared, but kept his voice even and his eyes steady. "I'm going to allow your present condition and your *former* reputation to cause me to forget you said that."

Denneval slumped. "I...I'm sorry, monsieur. I forget myself." He half raised his arm to signal for more wine, but hesitated and let it fall to the table. "I would like to have hunted with you, sir, in a better time and a better place."

"I'd have liked that too, monsieur."

The old wolf-killer drained the last of his glass and set the empty vessel down with a thump. "We'll be out of here within a week." He stood up unsteadily, and saluted the man across the table. "Good hunting, Antoine de Beauterne. May God be with you."

"And with you, monsieur," the younger man replied, acknowledging the salute. "Thank you."

Awkwardly sliding his chair aside with a loud scrape, Denneval d'Alencon, greatest hunter in France, killer of 12,000 wolves, shuffled out of the inn, slouching and defeated.

August 11, 1765

Antoine de Beauterne crouched on the muddy river-bank, inspecting the churned-up mire, the broken and matted reeds, the huge paw-prints that marked the passage of the Beast—or, at least, of *a* beast. They looked about right, though. Big, bigger than a wolf's would be—usually. He and his men had bagged some pretty big wolves out here in le Gévaudan; who knew how big a wolf could get if it had the rich diet this one seemed to prefer? He turned to the knot of people that stood watching him on the upper bank.

"And you didn't see it come back out of the water, mademoiselle?"

The young woman above him shook her head. She wore a bandage around one shoulder, through which a few small spots of blood seeped. "No, monsieur, I didn't. But I was busy tending to my sister. She'd come undone after seeing...after seeing the Beast, monsieur."

Antoine nodded and stood up, brushing his hands on the sides of his coat. He climbed back up the bank to where his huntsmen were gathered, along with the girl, Marie-Jeanne Valet. He gestured to a couple of his men. "Go take a look will you, upstream and downstream. I want to know where it came up. Or where its carcass washed up, God willing."

He turned back to the girl. "Now, mademoiselle, what makes you say 'Beast' like that? It wasn't a wolf?"

"Monsieur, that weren't no wolf I've ever laid eyes on, and I've seen plenty."

Antoine didn't doubt that she had; she was a strong young woman, this one. She was nervous and shaking, but not from fear. The nobleman knew the signs of the excitement that came after a hunt, the inflammation of the spirit that came from battling a wild animal in close quarters. God, these women of le Gévaudan were a tough bunch! With a grin, he continued his questioning. "Go on, please, mademoiselle. How was it different than a wolf?"

"Well, it was bigger than the biggest dog I've seen, for one, and it wasn't sort of...*taller* in front than behind. Like it was walking halfway like a human being, or something."

The hunting master glanced over to the man who stood near him. "Go on, please."

"Its head was huge, and sort of blunt. Not like a wolf's muzzle. And its mouth! It was wide and very black, but its teeth were beautiful white. It was white around its collar, too, then gray, then its back was black."

"You're sure about all that?"

"Well, if I may say so, monsieur, I saw it up real close."

"That you did, that you did." Antoine smiled at the bandage that wrapped her shoulder, and she blushed. He bent down and picked up a spear from the grass, the kind of improvised bayonet all the people of the region were carrying these days when they went out of doors, a big household knife lashed securely to a wooden staff. There were three inches of blood on the blade. "May I ask you to tell me again what happened here?"

"Of course, monsieur. Me and my sister came down here from Paulhac...that's the town just over the hill. Anyway, we came up to this fork in the stream and...well, that thing just came out of that thicket over there and jumped right on top of me. Got me good in the shoulder before...before I stabbed it, I suppose. I didn't think about it at all, just gave it everything I had. It pretty much pushed itself onto the knife, monsieur. It was real heavy."

Antoine watched her cheeks flush as she retold the story. What a girl this was! Tough, brave, skillful—the true heart of French womanhood. He made a note to himself to see she got the recognition she deserved, and continued the questioning. "And then what happened, after you stabbed the Beast?"

"Oh, it thrashed around and howled something fierce, monsieur. Grabbed at the wound with a front paw like a man would if he got stabbed. It rolled around a bit—you saw, there, where the grass was flattened—and then sort of half-ran, half-tumbled into the river. That's the last I saw of it, monsieur. Thérèse was screaming to wake the dead, so I went to her."

Antoine nodded and jotted a note in his little book. "Well done, mademoiselle. Well done, indeed!" The girl blushed again, deeper this time, and gave a very clumsy but honest curtsey. "You may have done a great thing for all your people, if your spear found its mark."

One of the men he'd sent out was riding back now. "Well?" he asked, as they trotted up.

"About a quarter mile upstream, on the other bank, sir," the rider answered.

"Any blood?"

"Didn't see any, sir, but that don't mean anything. We ought to bring some of the dogs out and see what they come up with."

Antoine nodded, making another note in his book. One more piece of information, one more mark on the map—soon he'd have the mind of the Beast, its patterns in his pocket. "There's no hurry. If it's not too injured, it'll be long gone by now. If this brave young lady wounded it mortally, it hardly matters if we find its body an hour from now or a day from now."

The Master of the Hunt swung up into his saddle, and gave the girl a jaunty salute as he turned his horse. "God be with you, mademoiselle. You have His Majesty's gratitude!"

Marie-Jeanne Valet was still blushing when the gallant hunter and his men disappeared over the hill.

August 16, 1776

Another day, another one of His Majesty's glorious hunts, thought 60-year-old Jean Chastel bitterly, leaning back against a tree with his gun across his lap. The way he figured it, the men of le Gévaudan could've caught their own Beast if the king would've just given them money, and maybe more guns. But no—there always had to be soldiers,

210 Werewolves and Shapeshifters

and fancy huntsmen, outsiders who need to be fed and watered and given the best of everything. Snobs who camped where they pleased and looked down on men who were born here and knew these hills backward and forward in a snowstorm at midnight. These fancy hunters figure the men of le Gévaudan are good for nothing but beating bushes or maybe, if they were good enough shots, waiting in one spot for hours as he was doing now, just in case the Beast decides to jump out and say hello.

Chastel spit on the ground. That old Norman fellow was at least bearable—with a couple thousand men tramping through the woods, it used to be pretty easy to avoid hunt duty without anyone noticing. Now it was harder. Didn't make any difference, though—kids were still dying, eight or nine since this Antoine de Beauterne started running the show. To top it all off, it looked like the rain was going to start up again.

The brooding man heard his son, Antoine, whistle for his attention from his post in a tree a few dozen yards away. "Hey, Papa! Look who's coming!"

Chastel stood and looked, and saw two of the royal huntsmen approaching. He had to admit they looked very noble and proud on their good horses, in their fine hunting livery. He looked nervously over at his son, who was grinning wickedly. Antoine was a troublemaker through and through, and a bad influence on his brother Pierre, who was posted just a few yards farther back. The old man had a bad feeling about this.

"Watch yourself, Antoine. Now's no time for trouble." Tensions were high everywhere in the region, among the soldiers no less than the peasantry. Fights were common, and the authorities—that is to say, Antoine de Beauterne and his captains —were running short of patience.

"Don't worry, Papa. I'll be friendly," his son said with a laugh as he swung out of the tree and stood casually on the path.

The riders drew up and hailed the family of gunners. "You there!" called the taller man in yellow, gesturing up at the way ahead, a marshy path that ran straight between two dense stands of trees. "Is that way not too boggy to ride through?"

The elder Chastel prayed in vain that his son might watch his tongue for once. "That way, good sir?" Antoine replied in his best imitation of fine speech. "Why, sir, it's as sound as any of His Majesty's royal highways! Ride right on through. And, if I may be so bold as to say, you might want to put a little speed on. Your noble fellow-hunters are quite some time ahead of you."

"Thank you, good man," the tall rider replied, kicking his horse into a fast trot. He pulled ahead of his more cautious companion in blue, who had to rein in sharply as the hunter in yellow and his horse plunged into a bog. Antoine and Pierre laughed like braying donkeys.

"Ha! Look, the mighty hunter reads the lay of the land!"

"Hey, I thought the Beast was a wolf, not a frog! Why are you hunting in the marsh?"

The two were laughing hysterically as the soldier in blue rode up and leaped off his horse, rushing forward to seize Antoine by the collar. "All right, you," he shouted, twisting the man's shirt. "You're coming with..."

His sentence was interrupted by a vicious punch from Pierre which sent him reeling. There was no laughing now, as Antoine whirled around with a snarl and raised his gun, pointing it square at the fallen huntsman.

"You want to try that again, fancy man?" There was death in his eyes, and the barrel of the gun quivered as his hands shook in rage.

"That's enough! Put that gun down!" Antoine looked up to see that the hunter in yellow had managed to free himself his horse from the quagmire and grab hold of the elder Chastel. "You don't want to add any trouble beyond what you're already in."

Pierre now raised his own gun, pointing it at the man who held his father. "What do you know about trouble?" he shouted. "You want to learn about trouble? You keep your hand on that old man one more instant, and you'll know all about trouble. Now take your friend here and ride! Solid ground's on the right."

The two hunters quickly beat their retreat under the threatening guns of the Chastel brothers, swearing all kinds of retribution—legal, physical and spiritual. Antoine just laughed after them in his braying way.

"Ha ha! Did you see the looks on their faces, Papa! Ha!"

"I saw it. You know what else I see? A nice long stay in prison, you idiot!"

Antoine looked sheepish for a second, then spit on the ground before looking up at the clouds with an air of speculation. "Well, at least that means we won't have to do anymore damned hunting for a while."

September 23, 1765

The back room of the chateau Antoine de Beauterne was using as his headquarters was dark in the daytime, shuttered and barred by his order. It also stank to high heaven, courtesy of the huge, hairy carcass that lay on a table in the center of the chamber. The buzz of flies greeted the Master of the Hunt when he entered carrying a lamp, followed by another man, bent and tottering with age but with hands strangely smooth and young-looking.

"Well. There it is, eh, monsieur?" asked the man, Antoine's personal taxidermist by appointment. He'd been in the hunter's service for years, mounting all his prize trophies. He did excellent work.

"There it is."

"The Beast, you say?"

"The Beast."

"Hm." The taxidermist had already begun inspecting the dark-furred body with professional interest, checking for damage to the hide which he'd have to conceal when mounting the specimen. He lifted a huge forepaw, noting the bloody wound there on the shoulder in addition to the obvious hole in the belly.

"Wounded it first, eh, monsieur? Was it you that got the kill?"

"No, mine was the shoulder. Rinchard took it in the belly as it was almost upon me. What do you think of it?"

"Big. Really big. Where did you take it?"

"Near the Abbey of Chazes, in an apple orchard. We tracked it after a report from a woman who'd driven it away from her baby with a bayonet. Excellent stock, these women, really; I'm surprised the Beast took any children at all, with such fierce mothers around."

"Indeed, monsieur, these hills breed them tough, just like this old girl here. An excellent specimen, truly."

"Thank you. Now, His Majesty is expecting the arrival of his trophy on or soon after the first of October. Can you have it ready by then?"

"Well, yes, monsieur, of course, but..." the old taxidermist's eyes had a strange little gleam in them in the lamplight. "Well, if monsieur doesn't mind me saying so, His Majesty already has a good number of trophy wolves, even ones as large as this."

"Ah, but I told you, sir, that this is not a wolf. This is the Beast of le Gévaudan. It is dead and the children are safe, and the flocks are secure and we can all go home and tell stories about it."

The wizened old coot looked back to the buzzing corpse on the table and raised his eyebrows with exaggerated interest. "Oh? I beg you pardon, monsieur, but that there looks like a big old she-wolf to me."

"I know it does. And that's a problem. Do you understand?"

The taxidermist smiled, showing his few crooked teeth. He was an artist, and he relished the rare chances when he really got to use his talent. "Oh, yes, monsieur, I understand perfectly. Now, if I might give you a list of supplies I'll need, I can get to work this very afternoon..."

June 19, 1766

Not for the first time, Jean Chastel cursed the name of Antoine de Beauterne. *I really believed he'd done it*, the old man thought with bitterness. When first word came that Antoine had killed the Beast, Chastel was just happy to be freed from prison—the stipulation of the sentence was that he and his sons would remain locked up until the

Master of the Hunt and his men were well clear of le Gévaudan. But when a week went by without a child killed, he felt a glimmer of hope. When two weeks had gone by, he felt more than a glimmer. When a month had gone by, he was certain—Antoine de Beauterne had bagged the Beast! It was worth a month in jail to see children walking without spears.

But then, come March of this year, the nightmare had started all over again. A boy at Montchauvet, a girl at Licones, an even younger girl at la Pouze—the Beast was back, if it had ever been gone. The king, of course, sent no noble hunters *this* time—he'd already paid out a fancy medal and a big pension to the great hero, Antoine de Beauterne, and he had the Beast stuffed in his parlor, or wherever. No, this time men of le Gévaudan were on their own, as maybe it should have been all along. The young Marquis d'Apcher, who was loved by most everybody, had no trouble organizing hunting parties—after two years of this, every man in the district was an old hand. And so old Jean Chastel found himself once again leaning against a tree, waiting for a bloodthirsty killer to make its appearance.

Maybe the old bishop was right, maybe they were all under a curse they could only pray their way out of. Well, old Jean came prepared for that too. He pulled out his little prayer book and began passing the time begging the Blessed Virgin to intercede on behalf of all those poor souls—his, included—who trembled in fear of this demon that walked among them. He had been praying for some time when he heard a rustling in from the brush at the far side of the clearing.

He glanced up and saw a huge black head, twice as wide as a dog's, emerging from the green, pushing before it a gleaming grate of bright white teeth. A strange calm came over him, and he bent his head back to his prayer book to complete his devotion. He knew he would be protected. And besides, he had prayer in a more physical, practical form—three small medallions of Our Lady: one for the Father, one for the Son and one for the Holy Ghost, specially cast into the musket ball that lay waiting in his gun. He could hear the Beast breathing, its footsteps drawing nearer.

With his final *amen*, Jean Chastel gently closed the prayer book, replaced it in his pocket and looked up once again. The Beast was a few long paces away—or one quick leap, if the reports were true. With slow, deliberate movements, he brought his gun around to bear on the hideous face that stalked toward him. Gently, he pulled the trigger and in a roar of thunder the musket discharged its holy payload, and put the Beast out of le Gévaudan's misery forever.

Jean Chastel was never properly rewarded for his kill; by the time he managed to bring his own trophy to Louis XV's attention, it wasn't much more than a pile of rotting meat. But he is remembered by many as the man who killed the Beast, and his musket is still on display as a memento of that time.

The End